The Tao of Yiquan:
The Method of Awareness in the Martial Arts

Volume 2 of the Trilogy

Warriors Of Stillness

Meditative Traditions
In The Chinese Martial Arts

by

Jan Diepersloot

The Tao of Yiquan:
The Method of Awareness in the Martial Arts

Volume 2 of the Trilogy
Warriors Of Stillness
Meditative Traditions In The Chinese Martial Arts

E-mail may be addressed to: jandiep@ncal.verio.com

Library of Congress Catalog Card Number: 99-90652

ISBN number: 96-49976-1-4

Book design and graphics by the author.

Gratefully Dedicated to

my friend and teacher
Sam Tam
for Showing the Way

and to

my sweetheart, my wife
Jean Vieth
for Support and Sharing

Acknowledgements

This book would not have become a reality without the help of a large number of people.

First and foremost, of course, I wish to express my deepest gratitude to my Yiquan teachers: Han Xingyuan, Yu Pengxi, Sam Tam and Fong Ha for their gracious sharing of this deep and ancient art.

Special thanks to Rita Townsend for her invaluable editorial assistance in turning my tortured prose into readable English. Also to Janet Russell for her superb indexing job, and Louis Swaim for help with the romanization of a number of Chinese terms and names.

Lastly, I want to thank the collective membership of Master Fong Ha's Saturday Berkeley Group and my own students for their continued support and stimulation. How blessed we are to be able to share these magnificent practices.

CONTENTS

CONTENTS

PART ii
The Life and Art of Wang Xiangzhai

PART iii
The Tao (Yang) of Yiquan

Chapter 6 Zhanzhuang and the Structure of Stillness

Chapter 7 Polarity and the Grammar of Movement

Chapter 8 Building Strength with Awareness

PART iv
The Tao (Yin) of Yiquan

Author's Introduction

The Warriors of Stillness trilogy is an account of a personal investigation into the three major meditative traditions in the Chinese martial arts: Taijiquan, Hsingyiquan, and Baguazhang. These arts can be thought of as sharing mutual points of departure and arrival, while differing in their means of transport. All three begin with stillness meditation as the cornerstone of their practice. They differ in the movements that derive from this stillness. But ultimately, in martial application, all these movements, like waves of the ocean, submerge again into a higher-level stillness.

In Volume 1, I presented the theory, practice and applications of standing meditation (wuji qigong) taught to me by my teacher Cai Songfang, as it relates to the movement of the Yang family style Taijiquan system. In this the second volume, I present the theory, practice and applications of standing meditation of the Yiquan branch of the Xingyiquan system as taught to me by my teachers Han Xingyuang, Yu Pengxi, Fong Ha and Sam Tam.[1]

It was Master Sun Lutan whose writings first grouped Taijiquan, Xingyiquan, and Baguazhang together as the neijiaquan or "internal family," as opposed to the "external schools" consisting of all other martial arts.[2] Since then, the martial arts community has seen endless acrimo-

---

[1] The trilogy will be completed with the publication, at a later date, of Vol. 3, which will present the essential theory and practice of Baguazhang. Additionally, audio-visual works on videos and CD will be released intermittently. If you would like to be informed when these products are published, please fill out the form on page 275 in the back of the book and return it to me.

[2] Sun Lutang, *Xing Yi Quan Xue:* The Study of Form-Mind Boxing, (Pacific grove, CA: High View Publications, 1993), p. 3.

i

nious debate over the definition and relative merits of internal versus external martial arts, as well as what school is or isn't internal or external. This debate, in my opinion, is largely spurious and evaporates when one takes the view that the relationship between external and internal martial arts describes the developmental process of mastery.

All martial arts, no matter what style the practice, start out being external because they use segmented strength and an excess of movement. The process of mastery is defined precisely by the mastery of the economy of movement and the transformation of external or segmented strength into internal or integrated strength. Taken to its highest artistic level, as the martial artist transforms all movement into stillness, the use of strength becomes invisible.

This is demonstrated not only by the masters of the internal schools, but also by the great masters of the so-called external styles such as Karate and many kinds of Gongfu. In truth, watching them work, one cannot differentiate them as external. They wait for their opponent to move first. When they touch, they move hardly at all and their opponent is defeated.

The uniqueness of the internal family schools of Taijiquan, Xingyiquan, and Baguazhang is not that only these schools produce masters of stillness. Rather, their uniqueness lies in the fact that right from the beginning they make the end product of the developmental process, stillness and awareness, the fundamental practice of their disciplines. Hence the trilogy's subtitle: "meditative traditions in the Chinese martial arts."

Author's Introduction

Part 3 of this second volume describes essentially the same meditative practices and results as described in Volume 1, but from a different perspective. It elucidates how the practice of stillness in standing meditation (1) defines and informs the use of movement of these arts and (2) is essential to developing peng (frame) and generating jin (explosive force).

Additionally, though, this second volume goes beyond Volume 1 in several significant respects. Parts 1 and 2 place the practices within a wider historical and cultural context. More importantly, Part 4 presents an entirely new dimension of development that has opened up to me as a result of my association with Master Sam Tam in the four years that have passed since the publication of Volume 1.

In my opinion, Sam Tam's achievement, developed logically from his practice of standing meditation, represents the highest phase of martial arts mastery. He has realized in his person the maxim that the slower we go, the more we can perceive. The achievement of great stillness generated great awareness in him. Moreover, he (re)discovered that with greater awareness less and less force is needed to control an opponent. His supreme artistry is to have honed this skill to such a phenomenal degree that he is able to control an opponent without any force whatsoever, but with his awareness alone. When an opponent attempts to engage him, all their strength and solidity dissolve into an emptiness that gently and inexorably overwhelms them.

THE TAO OF YIQUAN

My own involvement with these arts began in 1975 when a friend cajoled me into coming to one of his Taiji classes with Master Fong Ha in Berkeley. Little did I realize as we set out for the class that this encounter would become a critical turning point in my life.

Seeing Fong Ha move was a transcendent experience for me. As I watched I had a vision in which I saw myself in a future time moving like him, and like him, teaching by showing people the ancient rhythms of being and moving naturally. In a flash, then, my life took a new and entirely different direction.

The course seemed clear. I thought that with maybe ten years of hard practice I would be able to start teaching this art I had just fallen in love with. As it turned out, the time was somewhat shorter: six years later I began, however prematurely, to teach and to share my insights with others.

As in any transformational process, though, there were many ups and downs along the path. Soon after becoming Fong Ha's student, I had my initial moment of rude awakening, when preconceived notions had to be abandoned. First to go were all my ideas about movement and stillness and their relative importance in life and in the internal health and martial arts.

I had joined Fong Ha and his group for the quality of the movement. Yet only six months later, after a trip to Hong Kong, Fong came back and made the announcement that from now on the main practice would be a practice of stillness, not movement, called zhanzhuang, or standing as a stake or tree.

Author's Introduction

He further explained that zhanzhuang was the fundamental practice of a martial art called Yiquan, or Martial Art of the Mind, and that the name of his new teacher of this art was Han Xingyuan from Hong Kong. Master Han was a famous student of the founder of the Yiquan system, Grand Master Wang Xiangzhai, one of the most famous twentieth-century Chinese martial artists, whose main practice was simply standing still.

I was both appalled and intrigued—and rebellious, because I had signed on to really commit to the movement component of the internal arts and was now faced with the unwelcome prospect of constraining my movement into stillness. Fong's response, when I voiced my concern to him, was simply: "Why don't you try it (standing) for 100 hours and see what it feels like, then make a decision. Don't prejudge. Be open to new possibilities of experience."

That seemed fair, so I agreed to try for a 100 hours. Also, there was the element of intrigue. How could the mere practice of stillness generate such extraordinary athletic and martial skills? While this question brought out the old investigative journalist in me, I realized that to be able to write about it truthfully, I would have to submit myself to the experience.

And submit myself to the experience I did. During these past 25 years I've had the great fortune to study with four of the most highly regarded Yiquan teachers: Han Xingyuan, Fong Ha, Yu Pengxi, and Sam Tam. The contributions each of them have made to my total understanding of the Yiquan system will become clear as I relate my experiences with them. This book is a description of my experience with this art: what my teachers taught me, my breakthrough experiences, and an analysis of its inner structure and processes.

The book is, in a way, structured in reverse order from my personal experience with Yiquan. Whereas in life I first learned the art and then investigated its origins, the book will begin with an account of Yiquan's origins in ancient India. Then I tell of its migration, transformation and transmission in China. Lastly, I recount how my own teachers in the United States bequeathed its essentials to me.

Part 1

Buddhism and Martial Arts
in Ancient Asia

Chapter 1

Bhuddism and Martial Arts in Ancient India

1. Pre-Buddhist India

The social structure of ancient India was a rigid five-tiered caste system. The priests and teachers of the Brahmin caste wielded spiritual power. The warriors and rulers of the Ksatreya caste exercised temporal power. Farmers, merchants and artisans belonged to the Vaisya caste. Regular laborers constituted the Sudra caste. Lowest in the social hierarchy were the outcasts of the "untouchables" caste.

The Buddha's parents belonged to the Ksatreya caste. The Buddha, in other words, was born a prince into the ruling class of the India of his times.[1] Ksatreya culture was organized into clans, families, and groups that largely dedicated themselves and their arts, civil and martial, to larger spiritual goals. As a consequence, the Ksatreya culture had a highly developed ethical code, significant parts of which were later adopted by both the medieval knights of Europe and the samurai in Japanese culture.[2]

Military organization consisted of four classical divisions: chariots, elephants, cavalry, and foot soldiers.[3] According to their nature, each had different weapons and practice routines. Weapons used by Ksatreya in armed combat and training were various. Most widely used was the vajra, a mace or war club, the spiked variety

> The Buddha's parents belonged to the Ksatreya caste. The Buddha, in other words, was born a prince into the ruling class of the India of his times.

3

of which was also referred to as a "thunderbolt."[4] A variety of other weapons, such as spears, slingshots, and bows and arrows were also widely used in training and combat.[5]

Fig. 1-1. Nataraja -Deity of Martial Arts and Forms making circular movements.

The Ksatreya culture had a highly developed ethical code, significant parts of which were later adopted by both the medieval knights of Europe and the samurai in Japanese culture.

For unarmed fighting the Ksatreya caste developed a system of hand-to-hand combat called vajramukti,[6] meaning "thunderbolt fist." Vajramukti combined techniques of wrestling, throws, and hand strikes, along with tactics of movement and evasion to evolve a complete system of

Chapter 1 Martial Arts in Ancient India

unarmed combat. In peacetime training, vajramukti practice utilized sequences of attack and defense called nata in Sanskrit.[7]

In ancient Hinduism, the pursuit of nata, as a body-mind unification method was acknowledged as a spiritual study: the ruling deity, named Nataraja *(Fig. 1-1.)*, represents the awakening of wisdom through physical and mental concentration.[8] The deity was often depicted exhibiting the fundamental vajramukti pair of mudras (hand positions). These were the mudras of (1) fearlessness and (2) of receiving the vow, later adapted by Buddhism for its own purposes.[9]

The mudra of fearlessness is usually made by the right hand, but sometimes with both hands, as in *(Fig. 1-2)*. The palms are held upright facing toward the front and with the fingers extended upward. This mudra represents a mental condition in which that which experiences fear no longer exists, and therefore was a prime choice to represent the principles of warriorhood or martial arts. Often the mudra was drawn representing a circular motion in front of the body, symbolizing that all and every attack was to be harmlessly directed away from it. The mudra of fearlessness, therefore, represents an ultimately unselfish form of self-defense.

Fig. 1-2. Hindu deity with Absence of Fear mudra

Fig. 1-3. Buddha with mudras of Absence of Fear and Receiving the Vow

The mudra of the vow, made by the left palm up at the left side *(Fig. 1-3.)*, represents the Buddha's promise and the Bodhisattva's vow. The Bodhisattva is an enlightened being who has vowed to keep on reincarnating until all beings have become enlightened.

Over time, the longer and more complex original nata forms were condensed into shorter sequences called pratima, meaning "shape" or "form." The movements of the early pratima consisted of simple exercises for health and self-defense designed to work on the student's mind, body, and breath equally and on how to channel them into specific patterns of simultaneous interaction.[10] As a way to spiritual self-realization, the central, interior purpose of the pratima was to enable the practitioners to reveal and recognize their sthana. By sthana was meant the totality of the practitioner's perceived "stances" or concurrent positions in regard to their self-understanding.[11]

The process through which the nata practitioner became fully aware of his stances lay in a form of self-awareness training called samasthana. This term, which literally means a "configuration" or "distinctive patterning or shape," was frequently used in the vajramukti tradition. It denotes a series of practices designed to blend, intermingle and then dissolve all the various attitudes and postures (sthana), both physical and mental, of the practitioner into the great unity of awareness in the experience of totality.[12]

6

2. Buddha's Childhood Training

The Buddha was born in 623 B.C.E. in the town of Lumbini in the foothills of the Himalayas in southwestern Nepal, some 200 miles southwest of the present-day town of Katmandu. Lumbini was a luscious garden city full of green and shady sal trees. According to legend, the Buddha's mother, Maya Devi, loved Lumbini for its great beauty, and on her way to her parents' home in Devadaha decided to take a rest there and enjoy its beautiful environs. While she was standing, spellbound by the natural splendor of Lumbini, she felt labor pains, and catching hold of a drooping branch of a sal tree, gave birth to him who was to become the Buddha, or enlightened one *(Fig. 1-4)*.

Fig. 1-4. Nativity Scene of the Buddha's Birth

According to his station, the Buddha began his training in the Pancavidya (Five Arts) of the Ksatreya when he was seven years old. It is recorded that his teachers were named Arata, Kalama, and Rudrakarama. Additionally, the famous nata Master Kshantideva instructed the Bud-

Fig. 1-5. Buddha as a young marksman

dha in nata fundamentals of the physical arts of boxing, grappling, gymnastics, and weaponry.[13] Under such expert guidance, young Shakyamuni became highly trained and skilled in the warrior arts, as befitted his status as son of and heir to the reigning monarch *(Fig. 1-5)*.

Tales of the Buddha's physical prowess abound. One account tells how when he was 10 years old, the Buddha hurled an elephant some distance with such power that local villagers used the depression made by its falling body afterward as a water channel. He also is said to have fired arrows with such power that one of them hit a rock and opened an artesian spring.[14]

3. Buddhism and Indian History

There were four great periods in Indian history during which monarchs ruled their realms according to Buddhist ethics. The first Buddhist ruler was King Asoka, who reigned from 269 to 232 B.C.E. He was followed by the Kushan dynasty which lasted from 100 B.C.E to 500 C.E..

Thirdly, there was the Gupta dynasty (400-700 C.E), which saw a Buddhist renaissance under the monarch Harsha. Sanskrit was revitalized and cultural arts, such as sculpture, temple architecture, art, drama, and Buddhist nata flourished in all their many forms.

The last Buddhist period in India was during the Pala dynasty which began around 750 C.E and lasted until destroyed by the Muslim invasions the following century.[15]

The brutal Muslim destruction of Hindu and Buddhist culture in India included the suppression of the Ksatreya art of nata. Its tradition was dispersed and many of its teachers slain. Denied their heritage, subsequent generations evolved in quite different directions, often finding inspiration in such things as folk dancing, in the process diluting the purity of their Ksatreya nata movement arts.

The brutal Muslim destruction of Hindu and Buddhist culture in India included the suppression of the Ksatreya art of nata.

Thus, while later Buddhist schools in India preserved many of the physically oriented, but statically performed, meditation exercises, the practical knowledge of their significance as components of kinetic Buddhist practices was for the most part lost.[16]

Some representations of Buddhist nata movements and positions were preserved pictorially in the mandalas of esoteric Buddhism, usually in the form of the Vajramukti or Vajrasahndi Bodhisattva holding his hand in the "vajra closed hands on guard" position. These form part of the mandala quarter ruled by the Amodhasiddhi Buddha. [17]

4. Buddhism and Martial Arts

The Buddhist form of vajramukti de-emphasized and delimited the martial component and emphasized the spiritual component of nata.

When Buddhism first came to influence in India circa 500 B.C.E., it changed the Hindu practice of vajramukti nata and adapted it to its own purposes. On a symbolic level, the deity Nataraja was converted to one of the four protectors of Buddhism, and was renamed Naryayana Deva, and said to be the protector of the Eastern Hemisphere of the mandala.[18]

On a practical level, the Buddhist form of vajramukti de-emphasized and delimited the martial component and emphasized the spiritual component of nata. For the same reason, the Buddhist form of vajramukti, unlike its Vedic-Hindu predecessor, was strictly limited to empty hand practices and forbade the monks to engage in any form of weaponry.[19] And in the development of the unarmed Bodhisattva Vajramukti, the health-giving aspects of the defense sequences (nata) were emphasized as fundamental for the spiritual quest of balancing the body and mind relationship.[20]

The Buddhist monk masters sought to channel the experience obtained from the practice of nata into spiritual goals. At the simplest level, the practice of pratima involved creating an internal mental drama within which practitioners visualized, and then warded off, various kinds of armed and unarmed attacks. Later the appropriate emotional responses, along with these attacks, would also be visualized. Then, practitioners would try to create an awareness of both their own and their attacker's mental and emotional states during the sequences. Not only would they "see" the movement, they would also mentally "feel" the intensity and the hatred involved in its creation. By meditatively observing their mental relationship to such experiences, students could develop a direct awareness of the nature and content of their personal sthana.[21]

Chronology of Chinese Dynasties

2000-1500 B.C.E.   Xia

1500-1000 B.C.E.   Shang

1000-770 B.C.E.   Western Zhou

770-476 B.C.E.   Eastern Zhou –Spring and Autumn Period

475-221 B.C.E.   Eastern Zhou –Warring States Period

221-207 B.C.E.   Qin

206 B.C.-24 C.E.   Western Han

25-220 C.E.   Eastern Han

220-280 C.E.   Three Kingdoms (Wei, Shu & Wu)

265-315 C.E.   Western Jin

317-420 C.E.   Eastern Jin

420-589 C.E.   Liang (Southern and Northern)

581-618 C.E.   Sui

618-907 C.E.   Tang

907-959 C.E.   Five Dynasties & Ten Kingdoms

960-1279 C.E.   Song

1271-1368 C.E.   Yuan

1368-1644 C.E.   Ming

1644-1911 C.E.   Qing

1912-1949 C.E.   Republic of China

1949-   People's Republic of China

Fig. 2-1. Chronology of Chinese Dynasties

Chapter 2

Buddhism and Martial Arts in Ancient China

1. Buddhism in Ancient China

Buddhism first spread from India into China in the beginning of the Christian Era during the Eastern Han Dynasty. Due to a fortuitous set of circumstances, it became the main religion of China in the centuries that followed. Not only did the ruling class in general, and in particular the Han emperors, embrace and propagate Buddhism, but the population at large was also receptive to its teachings. The indigenous religions of Taoism and Confucianism were in relative decline, as they no longer spoke appropriately to the spiritual needs of people in a society in chaotic transition.

Initially, Taoism easily accepted Buddhism. By the second century, the Buddha was worshipped along with Lao Tzu, and some even claimed the two were one and the same. Later, more fundamental differences were perceived. For example, whereas the Taoist pursued the physical immortality of the body, the Buddhist sought liberation from any and all physical bodies.[1]

Initially, Taoism easily accepted Buddhism.... Later, more fundamental differences were perceived.

Meditation practices, likewise, emphasized different aspects. Taoists tried to reduce their breathing to a minimum, while concentrating on the circulation and transformation of the body's inner breath, while Buddhists emphasized more regulated breathing and detachment from the workings of the body.

Socially, Buddhists preferred community effort, while Taoists were more oriented to the individual, the former holding to a common set of rules, or precepts, for conduct, the latter leaving it more to individuals to discover and articulate the rules according to which they conducted their lives.

By the third century Buddhism went its separate way from Taoism and began its own process of proliferation into different sects, or schools of thought and practice.

Thus, by the third century Buddhism went its separate way from Taoism and began its own process of proliferation into different sects, or schools of thought and practice. Seven of the eight branchings (Three Treatise, Mind Only, Precept, Pure Land, Huyan, Tantric, and Zen schools) that occurred had their roots in or near Chungnan mountain in western China. The eighth school of thought, the Tientai sect, originated on Henghsan and Tientaishan in southern and eastern China.[2]

By and large, the success of Buddhism in China was made possible by the breakdown of Confucian synthesis of thought and institutions in the latter half of the second century. During that time the lower classes and peasants were exploited mercilessly by four groups of oppressors: the entrenched great families, the eunuchs, the nouveaux riche, and the intelligentsia. The covert struggle between these groups for the waning power of the imperial throne broke out into open violence in 166 CE. The eunuchs moved against the intelligentsia in a series of acts of slander, massacre, and assassination that plunged Chinese civilization into moral and political chaos.[3]

Then Taoist rebels against the Confucian imperium rose up in the Yellow Turban rebellions of 184 and 189.[4] Quarreling factions of the imperial court momentarily united and millions of lives were lost as province after province was laid waste by the repression of the revolt.[5] The process of moral, political, and economic deterioration continued to work the ruin of a once great empire. By the beginning of the fourth century, the dominant dynasty had only a shadow of effective control over large areas ravaged by famine, plague, drought, and migrations of starving people.[6]

The collapse of the Confucian imperial order created the vacuum into which Buddhism flowed into China through the routes of trade and communication from the Indian kingdoms. Many of the missionaries came from one or another of the great trading centers of central Asia, such as Dunhuang in the northwest and Chang'An and Loyang in the southern Yangtse valley.[7]

The collapse of the Confucian imperial order created the vacuum into which Buddhism flowed into China through the routes of trade and communication from the Indian kingdoms.

The first great translations that made the Mahayana (the "wide" or Bodhisattva Buddhist path) accessible and reasonably intelligible to literate Chinese was the work of Dharmaraksa, in 286 C.E., an Indian born in Dunhuang who had spoken Chinese from childhood.[8] By about the year 300, there were over 180 Buddhist establishments in the northern capitals of Chang'an and Loyang, with a clergy of some 3700.[9]

In 311 C.E. the north was lost to invading Huns. The emperor led an exodus of ruling classes, ignominiously fleeing south, and the country was effectively split into two. A letter found in the ruins of a watchtower west of Dunhuang recorded the fall of the ancient Chinese capital of Loyang and other cities by the Huns: "And, Sir, the last emperor—or so they say—fled from Saragh (Loyang) because of the famine, and his palace and walled city were set on fire...so Saragh is no more, Ngap (the great city of Yeh), further north, no more!"[10]

Buddhism, accordingly, had to adapt itself to two evolving cultures in the north and in the south.[11] According to their structure and social influences, the northern and southern schools developed different approaches to Buddhist practice and progress toward enlightenment. The southern school, dominated by old imperial remnants of the hierarchy, favored the slow and gradual path,[12] leading to the development of "pure land" Buddhism. In the north, the Zen school of sudden enlightenment[13] reflected the more chaotic social climate of that area—rife with racial tensions and shifting alliances between Chinese and aliens, as well as between Chinese themselves.

Buddhism had the support and protection of a succession of autocratic rulers, and from the mid-fourth century there was an extraordinary growth of Buddhism at all levels.

Because Buddhism was not native, it was acceptable to the Hun conquerors of the north. As a consequence, Buddhism had the support and protection of a succession of autocratic rulers, and from the mid-fourth century there was an extraordinary growth of Buddhism at all levels.[14] The rulers and their families supported a veritable orgy of building extravagant temples and monasteries, such as Shoalin, Loyang, and the cave temples at Dunhuang.

Since Buddhism had gained such a wide following among both peasantry and elite in north and south alike during the period of societal chaos, it became the obvious instrument for the subsequent reunification of north and south by the reunifying dynasty of Sui. [15]

2. Bodhidharma: The Founder (520 C.E.)

Undoubtedly the most famous and influential Indian/Buddhist missionary to China was the Bodhidharma, also known as Ta Mo, or Daruma (498-561 C.E.). Ta Mo arrived in China around 520 C.E. in the midst of an unprecedented period of Buddhist expansion and growth. For example, in the seven decades from 477C.E.to 534 C.E., the number of registered monasteries increased from some 6500 to over 30,000.[16]

In India Ta Mo was the twenty-eighth Buddhist Patriarch and in Chinese tradition he became the First Patriarch. When Ta Mo arrived in China he was right away summoned to an audience with Emperor Wu Di of the Liang dynasty at Nanking. The encounter of the Emperor and the Indian Prince-Bodhisattva was not a fruitful one; there was no "meeting of the minds." Ta Mo was unable to convince the emperor of the validity of his doctrine of "sudden" as opposed to "gradual" enlightenment.

Fig. 2-2. Ta Mo

Ta Mo then left for the Song Mountains, travelling until he reached the original Shaolin (Little Forest) Monastery, a temple originally founded in 490 C.E. by Emperor Xiao Wen for Ta Mo's predecessor, the Sarvastivada monk Ba Tuo. [16] It was there that his teachings began to take root and to spread throughout northern China.

During the preceding five centuries there had been a gradual divergence of teachings and practices between the Indian and Chinese forms of Buddhism. One of the main differences appeared to center on the mind-body relationship. In India, under the influence of Hindu yogic practices, Buddhism, while emphasizing the pre-eminence of the mind, also stressed the cultivation of the body and its well-being to make it a suitable dwelling place for the mind.

In China, on the contrary, the cultivation of the body had been entirely neglected in favor of the exclusive cultivation of the mind. The Chinese Buddhists had begun to refer to the body in derisive terms as a "notorious skin bag," the predictable result being that as a rule the practitioners' state of physical well-being degenerated and became lamentably bad.

When Ta Mo arrived at Shaolin Monastery, the monks had been practicing austere long-term meditation retreats. Bodhidharma, in true Mahayana spirit, was moved to pity when he saw their terrible physical condition. Likening them to the young Shakyamuni—who, as legend has it, almost died from such ascetic practices— Bodhidharma sequestered himself in a cave to contemplate the problem and find a solution. [17]

During the five centuries from 0-500CE there had been a gradual divergence of teachings and practices between the Indian and Chinese forms of Buddhism

When he emerged from the cave after nine years, he informed the monks that he would teach their "bodies and minds" the Buddha's dharma. To this end he taught them one complete nata and two pratimas of the Bodhisattva Vajramukti practice, namely the nata of Buddhist Lion Play School and two of its pratimas (shorter sequences).[18]

The nata was called the Astadasajacan or Astadasavijaya, which translated literally means the "Eighteen Subduings" or "Eighteen Victors." As these Indian concepts and teachings were absorbed by Chinese culture, these practices came to be called the Shiba Luohan Shou, or the "Eighteen Hand Movements of the Immortals (Arahants)."[19] A single Chinese term, xing, served as translation of both nata and pratima. And so the xing of the Shiba Luohan Shou (in its long form) was composed of eighteen classical sets of mudra or hand gestures.[20]

Fig. 2-3. Ta Mo's cave

Each of the mudras was combined with respiratory patterns, steps, muscle flexations and specific meditation themes. The Shiba Luohan Shou was the most important Buddhist nata/xing introduced into China and the foundation of what is now known generically as the Shaolin Szu school of martial arts, or Quanfa, [21]which will be described more fully in the following section. Shiba Luohan Shou has been variously translated as "Eighteen Buddha Boxing Methods," or "Eighteen Ways of the Warrior Monks." At it deepest levels, this Buddhist martial art bequeathed by Bodhidharma pertained to three levels of understanding and meaning relating to mind, body, and speech analysis common in both the esoteric and exoteric schools of Buddhism.

Shiba Luohan Shou has been variously translated as "Eighteen Buddha Boxing Methods" or "Eighteen Ways of the Warrior Monks."

The two shorter forms (pratimas) of this xing (nata) which the Bodhidharma also taught were (1) the Asthimajja Parisuddhi —a Buddhist movement and respiratory yoga for tissue regeneration, catharsis, and karmic recognition, and (2) the Snavasjala Nidana Vijnapti—a special and cathartic physical discipline of psychic energy purification through mantra and meditation.[22]

The Chinese term for Asthimajja Parisuddhi was Xisuijing, meaning "Bone Marrow Washing." The Chinese term for Snavasjala Nidana Vijnapti was Yijinjing, or the "Sutra (teaching) for the Conditioning of the Tendons and Ligaments." As these physical practices taught by Bodhidharma were absorbed into Chinese culture, beginning as early as the twelfth century, many Taoist manuscripts were produced that were imitations of these Buddhist classics. As a result, depending on your perspective, there occurred a profound cross-fertilization, or contamination. Most versions available today, although sometimes very old, are often Taoist or folk compositions containing sequences different from those taught by the Bodhidharma and sometimes lacking the spiritual component of Indian origin.[23]

20

Chapter 2 Buddhism And Martial Arts In Ancient China

In the spiritual realm, Bodhidharma expounded the sutras (teachings) of Mahayana (Great Vehicle) Buddhism in such a way as to emphasize the dual cultivation of mind and body by means of the balanced practice of stillness meditation (jing gong) and movement meditation (dong gong). In accord with traditional practice, Bodhidharma continued to teach the cultivation of the mind by means of the practice of stillness in sitting meditation. Through the practice of the Buddhist martial arts, theYijinjing and the Xisuijing, the monks at Shoalin temple, under the tutelage of Bodhidharma, soon began to reintegrate their bodies with their minds.

Through the practice of the Buddhist martial arts, the Yijinjing and the Xisuijing, the monks at Shoalin temple, under the tutelage of Bodhidharma, soon began to reintegrate their bodies with their minds.

TheYijinjing, utilizing a type of isometrics alternating tension and relaxation within given postures and movement, changed their physical health from poor to excellent. Not only that, but they found that their physical strength became greatly enhanced. TheYijinjing stretched the muscles, ligaments and tendons of their entire bodies in such a manner that it made them both extremely supple and strong while generating abundant qi or vital energy.[24]

TheXisuijing in addition taught the monks how to use their qi to strengthen the blood and the immune system, as well as the central nervous system. Thus a healthy body and brain contributed significantly to their progress in attaining mental enlightenment and peace of mind.[25] One of the unfortunate consequences of the subsequent neglect of Ta Mo's teachings was that the Xisuijing, or bone marrow washing teachings, was all but lost. Current knowledge of them is based mostly on ancient descriptions, and only a few fragmentary movements and their underlying concepts have filtered down to us through the ages.

Fortunately, the Yijinjing set of exercises escaped this fate. Undoubtedly largely due to its amazing potential to transform weak muscles, ligaments and tendons into unusually strong and resilient ones, it was picked up by many martial arts traditions. These traditions existed mostly inside the minority of Buddhist monasteries that continued to adhere to Ta Mo's teachings of unity of body and mind, such as the famous Shaolin Monastery, but also outside of them in independent currents.

Each martial art which incorporated the Yijinjing practice modified it to suit its own needs. Consequently, a great variety of different versions of the Yijinjing have come down to us in its transmission over time from generation to generation. To many qigong scholars, practitioners and medical doctors, the version recorded and preserved in the Qing Dynasty (1644-1911 C.E.) Imperial Annals is probably the most authentic version, closest to the original teachings of Ta Mo.

The Tang dynasty in China lasted from 600-900 CE. It was primarily a Buddhist one, and ... a remarkably peaceful period.

3. Tang Dynasty (600-900 C.E.): Martial Art as Spiritual Quest

The Tang dynasty in China lasted from 618-907 C.E. It was primarily a Buddhist one, and despite the sharpening of the distinctions between the southern (gradual) and northern (sudden) schools of thought, it was a remarkably peaceful period. It was a time that saw a great flowering of Indian Buddhist physical/mental culture,[26] including the spread of vajramukti nata, which contained the principles of health preservation, teachings of weaponless self-defense, and meditative insight.

As the monk teachers of the Tang Dynasty began to incorporate the Indian imports into existing Chinese traditions, Vajramukti was taught under the Chinese name of Quanfa. Like the Indian word vajra, the actual Tang Chinese character "quan" means closed or clasped hand or fist. The suffix "fa" was the Chinese transliteration of the Sanskrit term dharma (teachings of Buddha). Such a suffix was commonly used throughout Chinese Buddhism to represent not just the teachings themselves, but all the arts, crafts, and practices associated with them. Like Vajramukti, Quanfa then means roughly the thunderbolt, or closed hand (fist) of the dharma, or teachings of Buddha.[27]

Fig. 2-4. Tang Dynasty Buddha

Quanfa was taught only to devout Buddhists or monks. As a spiritual discipline, Quanfa seeks to integrate the body/mind interaction so that by transforming the body one is freed from the body and by transforming the mind, one is freed from the mind. This was called "exchanging one's body for that of the Buddha," and results in a condition of non-self being (naitratmyacitta; chin: wuxin).[28]

By the practice of this nata, or xing, monks sought to attain the paradoxical body-mind relationship defined by dynamic stillness and a stilled dynamic. Through such a realization the highest mental liberation in, and of, mind and body could be attained. This transformation was the real significance of the Sthana and Samastanha principles in the art of Quanfa and the real goal of the kinetic sequences.[29]

Fig. 2-5. Tang Dynasty
Celestial Warrior (1)

The goal of Xingyi (samasthana), or self-awareness training or quest of Quanfa, was to gain complete mastery over the active processes that gave rise to the various forms of suffering engendered, experienced, and perpetuated, often unknowingly, by the practitioner. Within this context, the motivation to protect oneself in the way we usually understand this act is not found in Quanfa. Rather, Quanfa proceeds from the more basic spiritual premise that personal self-defense is ultimately pointless, and only the opportunity to help or teach others exists continually. If in the face of aggression one can avert harm to oneself or others, an opportunity to teach the aggressor is created.[30]

During this period of Buddhist growth during the Tang dynasty, the monk was regarded as a spiritual warrior who engaged in battle between his higher and lower natures on the battlefield of the monk's mind, speech, and body. Taking account of this trinity of mind, speech, and body, the xing developed a shorter name, based on an abbreviation of Sanskrit titles, namely "triple battle" or trican in Sanskrit. In Chinese this became sanjin or sanchan, which also became the name of the predominant stance or posture of this xing.[31]

In the xing of sanjin the arms are placed in the mudra of the Vajramukti Bodhisattva portrayed in the Kongokai Maha Mandala, and this whole position is known as the Trilokavijayakayaasthana, meaning the position of one who has subdued the three realms of existence. It is taken from the outer shape of the vajra

Fig. 2-6. Tang Dynasty Warrior (2)

(thunderbolt) and physically embodies its triangulation of physical and mental harmony and balance. In this stance the body is segmented into five elemental levels, each composed of three equal degrees of torsion. These form three complete "jewel" shapes representing the Buddha, Dharma, and Sangha. [32]

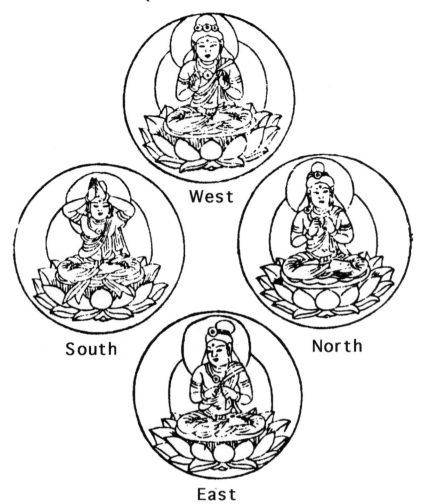

West

South

North

East

Fig. 2-7. Kongokai Maha Mandala

By balancing the tripartite torsion, both in the outer muscles and the inner organs, a composite pattern of physical power is maintained in which the body, although totally stilled, is capable of instantaneous responses to external conditions. The sanjin posture is non-aggressive in appearance, and when wearing a monk's robe, is completely invisible to the outside observer. It is also the only stance from which a monk can immediately stand or sit in the cross-legged meditation position. [33]

Chapter 3

The Secularization of Buddhist Martial Arts

1. Song Dynasty (960 -1279 C.E.)

In the later years of the Tang dynasty, the pendulum once again began to swing the other way, as those in power wanted to curtail the success of Buddhism for their own political reasons. The Song dynasty went even further, returning to an explicit neo-Confucian code of ethics, and in the process Buddhism was increasingly weakened as it was appropriated by the native traditions.[1] Due to lack of patronage, many of the great and imposing Buddhist temples fell into ruins, a fate bemoaned by an ancient poet:

> No monk lives at the old temple,
> The Buddha has toppled to the floor;
> One bell hangs high, bright with evening sun,
> Sad that when only a tap is needed,
> No one now dares to rouse the notes of
> Solemn music that cram its ancient frame.[2]

The Song dynasty was a sorrowful time in China: corruption in business and government, natural calamities, and mass starvation defined it as a period of continued cultural, political, and spiritual deterioration.

Indeed, the Song dynasty was a sorrowful time in China. Corruption in business and government, natural calamities, and mass starvation defined it as a period of continued cultural, political, and spiritual deterioration.[3] This process culminated in the effective splitting of the country into two parts when the north was once again invaded and seized, this time by the Jin, in 1127 C.E.. This date became the line of demarcation between the northern Song (960-1127 C.E.) and the southern Song dynasties. (1127-1279 C.E.)[4]

27

Fig. 3-1. Shaolin temple

Historically, the popularity of the martial arts in China has waxed and waned depending on the relative stability, peace and prosperity in society. In periods of turmoil and transition, the martial arts expanded and developed. In periods of greater social cohesion, they declined. Thus it is no surprise that during the turmoil of the Song dynasty, the martial arts flourished and proliferated. The Shoalin monastery, for example, reached the height of its fame during the Song when it boasted over 2000 resident monks.[5]

During those times, the Buddhist Shaolin temple martial arts began to proliferate beyond the gates of the temple. This resulted in both the secularization of the art and its fragmentation into numerous specialized systems. The following list, though only partial, illustrates the wide

Fig. 3-2. Shaolin temple

variety of martial arts systems that spun off the original Buddhist Shaolin Quanfa: Eighteen Lohan Hands, Eighteen Lohan Quan, Eighteen Lohan Palm, Big Hongquan, Small Hong Quan, Continuous Quan, Six Harmony Continuous Quan, Five Animal Quan, Snake Quan, Tiger Quan, Dragon Quan, Panther Quan, Crane Quan, Chao Yang Quan, Plum Blossom Quan, Nine Quans, Lohan Quan, Cannon Quan, Tongbi Quan, Tongbi Continuous Quan, Long Quan, Eagle Quan, Changchui Quan, Jingang Quan, Six Harmony Quan, Black Tiger Quan, Seven Star Quan, Shaolin Short Hitting, Five Harmony Quan, Chuojiao Quan, Tiangang Quan, Rock Quan, Xinyi Quan, Eight Extremequan, Hungry Tiger Quan, Fire Dragon Quan, Golden Rock Quan, Fierce Tiger Quan, Kanjia Quan, Eight Step Continuous Legs, Exiting Mountain Quan, Scissor Quan, Reverse Arm Quan, Six Ancestor

During the turmoil of the Song dynasty, the martial arts flourished and proliferated.

29

Quan, Soft Quan, Monkey Quan, Shaolin Quan, Taijiquan, etc....[6]

2. Shaolin Ethical legacy

If in leaving the temples and being claimed by the world, the Buddhist martial arts were secularized, the secular world of martial arts was being subtly civilized by the Buddhist ethical code. In the words of the Chinese Internal arts Master Hong Yixiang, it was Ta Mo and his followers who introduced wute, or martial virtue: "Prior to the arrival of Ta Mo, Chinese martial artists trained primarily to fight and were fond of bullying weaker folk. Ta Mo brought wute, which taught that the martial arts are really meant to promote spiritual development and health, not fighting."[7]

Ta Mo brought wute, which taught that the martial arts are really meant to promote spiritual development and health, not fighting.

In the Shaolin Temple in the past, before a disciple was accepted, he had to swear a vow of obedience of the Moral Code, in front of Lord Buddha, his Master(s), and seniors. Though no doubt transformed and diluted from its original formulations, the Shaolin Moral Code continues to be handed down from generation to generation of Shaolin martial practitioners. It consists of three parts: (a) Shaolin Ethics, (b) Forbidden Acts, and (c) Obligations.[8]

Shaolin Ethics
- Respect the master, honor the Moral Code and love the fellow disciples.
- Train Gongfu devotedly and build up a strong healthy body.
- Forbidden to molest or rape; forbidden to go astray.
- Forbidden to show off the arts; nor to offend the seniors.

Chapter 3   The Secularization of Buddhist Martial Arts

• Forbidden to laugh for no reason; nor to tell lies.

• Forbidden to bully those under you; nor to take advantage of high office for settling personal differences.

• Forbidden to quarrel loudly, waving the hands wildly.

• Forbidden to kick about aimlessly, to stand at fighting stances, nor to make accusations against others noisily.

• Forbidden to spread false rumors; nor to boast of strength and oppress the weak.

• Forbidden to be greedy; neither to rob nor steal others' properties.

• Be humble and soft-spoken; be unbashful in seeking advice for knowledge.

• Develop self-control, be co-operative and helpful.

Forbidden Acts

• Forbidden to molest or rape.

• Forbidden to rob another person's wife; nor to force someone into marriage.

• Forbidden to bully the kind and gentle people.

• Forbidden to rob.

• Forbidden to take advantage of intoxication to do evil.

• Forbidden to torture; nor to be cruel.

• Forbidden to be involved in improper activities.

• Forbidden to show disrespect to the elders.

• Forbidden to rebel against the master.

• Forbidden to associate with villains.

Obligations.

• Obliged to eliminate the cruel and the villainous.

• Obliged to protect the lonely and the oppressed.

• Obliged to be chivalrous and generous.

• Obliged to right wrongs courageously.

• Obliged to spread Shaolin teachings and gongfu.

• Obliged to learn the Art for self-defense and to over come calamity.

• Obliged to pass on the Art unselfishly to selected, good disciples.

3. Yueh Fei and Xingyiquan

The one martial arts system on the list of Shaolin-derived martial arts that is of particular importance to our study is Xinyiquan, which in later times became more generally known as Xingyiquan. In English "xing" means form or configuration, "yi" means mind or intent, and "quan" means fist, boxing, or martial art. The literal meaning of the term Xingyiquan, then, is "the martial art of physical form and mind intent."

Yueh Fei based his Xingyiquan system precisely on the principles of the Buddhist Yijinjing, the specific and unique use of tension and relaxation.

Xingyiquan was synthesized from various martial arts by a famous general named Yueh Fei. More specifically, Yueh Fei based his Xingyiquan system precisely on the principles of the Buddhist Yijinjing, the specific and unique use of tension and relaxation described in Chapter 2. This method of training employed the principle of interpenetration or interdependence of the polarities of yin and yang, of using relaxation within tension and tension within relaxation. As his legacy to posterity, Yueh Fei left an illustrated manual on the walls of a temple on Zhongnan Hill.[9]

Born on Feb. 15, 1103 C.E. in Tang Yin Hsien, Henan province, Yueh Fei became a Chinese hero, a great scholar of the classics in peacetime and in wartime a brave and shrewd general. His initial martial arts teacher, who taught him the arts of the Shaolin temple, was named Jou

Ton. In 1122, at age 22, Yueh Fei joined the southern army of liberation. In the ensuing years, he diligently worked himself up through the ranks until he became commanding general. He then instituted a systematic training program of internal and external martial arts. With his armies thus trained, Yueh Fei skillfully defeated the enemies of his country numerous times, as the south attempted to liberate its lost lands.[10]

His "Ten Theses on Xingyiquan" demonstrates profound understanding, showing the correct way to master the art. Yueh Fei compiled and organized Xingyiquan into an effective system to train his soldiers and is believed to be the first person to take the secrets of Xingyiquan outside the Shaolin monastery and reveal them to the public at large. He also created the external style known as Yueh's Family Eagle Claw style. An expert in Chinese medicine, Yueh Fei was also a qigong master credited with creating the Eight Pieces of Brocade exercise set.[11]

Fig. 3-3. Yueh Fei

In the end, however, Yueh Fei himself fell victim to the corruption of his times. After scoring a decisive military victory against the northern Jin conquerors, his enemies successfully bribed one of the emperor's corrupt officials. As a result, the Emperor then had Yueh Fei recalled to the capital and imprisoned him until he died in jail in 1142 C.E.. In 1166 C.E. Emperor Xiao Zong rehabilitated Yueh Fei and relocated his grave to the beautiful West Lake (Xi

Hu) in Hangzhou. The emperor gave him a new name: Yueh Wu Mu, or Yueh, the righteous and respectable warrior.[12]

4. Buddhism, Taoism and the Creation of Hsingyiquan

Yueh Fei's creation of Xingyiquan is an interesting study of the melding of the Indian Buddhist tradition and native Taoist tradition. In both name and form, the original Indian/Buddhist tradition is clearly discernible, whereas in content, a Taoist layer of interpretation was superimposed.

Yueh Fei's creation of Xingyiquan is an interesting study of the melding of the Indian Buddhist tradition and native Taoist tradition.

The name Xingyi, as Sifu Nogaboshi demonstrates, is the exact Chinese translation for the Indian term samasthana,[13] denoting the discipline of discovering and transforming one's self through practice and insight into one's physical and spiritual postures. Moreover, Hsingyiquan also became known as Wuxing or Five-Element Fist, which Nogaboshi likewise traces back to the Indian Mahabhuta Nata or Five Great Elements Nata. This original martial arts routine concerned itself with emulating the principles of the five elements, which arose prior to, and independent of, similar Chinese preoccupations.

The fundamental practice of Hsingyiquan is in the "santi" or "trinity" posture, which is clearly derived from the fundamental Shaolin Quanfa posture known as sanjin, or "triple battle." But whereas their other forms came to vary somewhat, the inner purpose and principles of structural alignment of the santi and the sanjin postures remained identical.

34

Chapter 3   The Secularization of Buddhist Martial Arts

As far as the torso is concerned, both share an insistence on keeping the back straight from coccyx to the top of the head, eliminating the lumbar curve of the spine by use of the pelvic tilt and tucking the tailbone. Both insist that the transformational process of the body-mind must begin with the transformation of the normal pathological spine as represented by *Fig. 3-4.* into the natural spine as depicted in *Fig. 3-5.*

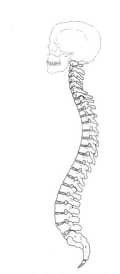 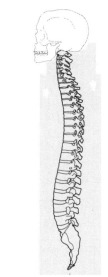

The transformational process of the body-mind must begin with the transformation of the normal, pathological, spine into the natural spine.

Fig. 3-4. Normal spine   *Fig. 3-5. Natural spine*

On the surface, the position of the feet seems to be quite contrary. In the sanjin stance, as still practiced today by many Chinese and Japanese martial arts, the front foot is toes in, while the rear foot is straight; and in the santi posture, the front foot is straight with the rear foot angled out. But in fact, the internal sensation of the santi posture, as described by Sun Lutan, is clearly expressed in the outer form of the sanjin posture: "the knees feel as though they are closing inward and the heels feel as if they are pushing outward, while the toes feel as if they are grasping the earth."[14]

Fig. 3-6. Sanjin feet

Fig. 3-7. Santi feet

"...the knees feel as though they are closing inward and the heels feel as if they are pushing outward, while the toes feel as if they are grasping the earth."

The position for the arms and hands most frequently utilized in the Quanfa sanjin is the mudra of the Vajramukti Bodhisattva portrayed in the Kongokai Maha mandala (Fig.2-7.), and known as the Triloavijanakayasthana or the position of one who has subdued the three realms of existence.[15] It is often represented in various forms by the attendants of the Buddha.

The Xingyi santi posture, as demonstrated here by Sun Lutang, is a clear echo of the mudra which "grants the absence of fear," often assumed by the Buddha himself in standing representations. The Buddha purportedly used it to subdue an elephant set upon him by one of his enemies.[16]

Fig. 3-8. Vajramukti
Bodhisattva

Fig 3-9. Buddha and
attendants

Finally, the sanjin and santi stances share a fundamental common purpose. Their practice leads to the state of nonanalytical thinking or "no-mindedness" which enables the individual to respond spontaneously in combat to the total configuration of the situation, rather than focusing on any single aspect of the opponent.

Fig 3-10. Sun Lutan
in Santi posture

In the interpretive dimension, we can see how native Taoist concepts replaced Indian ones. Sanjin was the Chinese translation for the Indian trican, which itself was an abbreviation and integration of the Sanskrit Astadsajacan and Triatyabhumi postural configurations, and which referred to the "triple battle" in the realms of mind, body, and speech the monk aspirant had pledged himself to.[17] This is still reflected in a Japanese legend concerning the basis of the sanjin stance that tells the story of "three mythological gods that were the finest fighters in China, who were only undefeatable when they were fighting together. These were the gods of the eyes (mind), of breathing (speech), and of posture (body)." [18]

In Xingyi, the santi or trinity posture refers to the macrocosmic trinity of heaven, earth, and man which, in Xingyi martial theory is represented microcosmically in the body of man as the head, hands, and feet. Each is further divided into three sections.[19] It is precisely this shift of interpretive emphasis that represents the superimposition of the Taoist cosmological world view onto the essentially Indian cosmology.

In Xingyi, the santi or trinity posture refers to the macrocosmic trinity of heaven, earth, and man, which, in Xingyi martial theory is represented microcosmically in the body of man as the head, hands, and feet.

In the words of an ancient Taoist classic: When yang and yin united, the three essentials were created, which in turn produced all creatures. Thus the one qi that came from the emptiness and created yang and yin is the foundation of heaven and earth, with man placed in the middle to serve as bridge and instrument of balance and unification. It is precisely this emphasis on the trinity of heaven, earth, and man that is typical of a Taoist world view and absent from Indian Hindu and Bhuddist cosmological schemes.[20]

Chapter 3 The Secularization of Buddhist Martial Arts

5. Yuan and Ming Dynasties (1271-1644 C.E.)

In the period that followed the turmoil of the Song Dynasty, namely the Yuan Dynasty (1271-1368 C.E.) and well into the Ming Dynasty (1386-1644 C.E.), scholars and educated people of the time emphasized the civil arts, such as politics and diplomacy. They avoided and belittled the martial arts and the great wisdom inherent in them. They contemptuously regarded the martial artists as bullies who only loved to compete, fight, and generally make trouble. And, it is only fair to note that despite the influence of Buddhist ethics, this assessment was correct more often than not.

The emphasis on the trinity of heaven, earth, and man is typical of Taoist world view and absent from Indian Hindu and Bhuddist cosmological schemes.

Not surprisingly, then, those who practiced the martial arts and understood the deep ethical and philosophical knowledge inherent in them, moved away from the power centers into small villages and monasteries, keeping to themselves and hiding their wisdom and knowledge from the general public. Thus the martial arts once again declined and most of their secret essence was lost from human awareness.

But in the late Ming Dynasty, with society once more in transition, the need for martial arts for self-defense and warfare once more resulted in their resuscitation. According to Wang Xuanjie, a native of Shan Xi by the name of Ji Jike (Ji Longfeng) rediscovered Yueh Fei's Illustrated Boxing Manual on the then broken down walls of the Zhongnan Hill Temple.[21] Yang Jwing Ming, on the other hand, writes that Ji obtained Yueh's manuscript, "a secret book on Xingyi", on Zhongnan Mountain.[22] Whatever the physical form, by studying the material intensively and practicing diligently, Ji Jike came to understand its profound implications and realized its power in his person. Thus he lay the foundations for the Xingyiquan of later times.

Ji Jike had two main disciples to whom he passed on the essence and totality of his art, Cao Jiwu and Ma Xueli. Ma Xueli went on to become the founder of the Honan School branch of Xingyiquan, while Cao Jiwu founded the Shan Xi School branch of Xingyiquan. [23]

6. Qing Dynasty (1644-1912 C.E.)

During the Qing Dynasty (1644-1911 C.E.), the brothers Dai Bengbang and Dai Longbang became the favored disciples of Cao Jiwu, inheriting the mantle of direct lineage succession.

Then a certain Li Luoneng from Hebei province heard rumors about the extremely high level of skill Dai Longbang had developed and went to study with him. At first, Dai Longbang apparently was quite stingy with his information, which only changed after Dai's mother intervened. "At a birthday party for Dai's mother, Li so impressed her that she berated her son for being so niggardly in his teaching. After that Dai taught Li the whole art, and Li mastered it at the age of forty-seven."[24]

As a result of his training with Dai Longbang, Li Luoneng became so skillful and powerful that he was called "divine fist." His skill and speed were so great that his opponents never had a chance to come close to him.

When challenged, he went forward easily, put out his hand and achieved his purpose. After he had completed his studies with Dai Longbang, Li Luoneng went back home to the province of Hebei, concentrating on training his disciples, with the result that his Henan branch of Xingyiquan became famous throughout China.

The most accomplished student of Li Luoneng was a man called Guo Yunshen, who became, if possible, even more famous than his teacher for his overwhelming power. The stories vary, but it appears Guo killed at least one man, and possibly several others, who came to challenge him. As a result he spent three years in prison restricted by fetters. One would think this would have been a severe impediment to his practice. But actually it proved a blessing in disguise.

Restricted from any movement, Guo developed Xingyiquan's deepest essence: the discharge of extremely powerful and explosive force from a still posture

Fig. 3-11. Guo Yunshen (In white Robe and black vest)

to new heights of sophistication.[25] So powerful was Guo's discharge of energy that some called him "Divine Crushing Hand," while others, less favorably inclined to him but equally impressed, called him "demon hand."

Apparently, however, prison did teach Guo that it was wiser not to kill his opponents. After his release, the story goes, Guo was always careful to place his left hand on his opponent's body, before issuing with his famous right hand.[26] The left hand helped absorb the energy of his right, thus preventing serious injury to his opponent. Needless to say, with the appearance of Guo Yun Shen on the martial arts scene, the fame of Xingyiquan as the ultimate boxing art spread far and wide throughout China.

7. Guo Yunshen's Summary of Xingyiquan [27]

"Xingyi is similar to Taoist meditation: both have the goal of emptiness. But where we go from inaction to action, the Taoists go from action to inaction. We borrow from the Taoists three changes: (I) sperm (sexual energy) to qi, (2) qi to spirit, and (3) spirit to emptiness.

Xingyi is similar to Taoist meditation. Both have the goal of emptiness. But where we go from inaction to action, the Taoists go from action to inaction.

"The way to mysterious (hua) energy is through the obvious and the concealed energies. To get obvious you must be centered and balanced. Through this energy sperm is worked into qi, which changes the bones. At birth our bodies are strong but later they decline. Ta Mo developed a teaching to change the sinews and to wash the bone marrow. He believed that this would permit the body to return to its prenatal state. In the Song dynasty (960- I 279), Yueh Fei added to Ta Mo's doctrine that of changing the bones. The Five Fowl exercise and Eight-Part exercise reflected these teachings. After concerted prac-

	Xingyi Stages	Sedentary Stages	Changes	Type of Energy	Type of Breathing
1	Change sperm into qi	Fire work (hard burning)	Bones	Overt	Basic
2	Change qi into spirit	Summoning fire	Sinews	Covert	Intermediate
3	Change spirit into emptiness	Divine fire	Marrow	Mysterious	Advanced

Fig. 3-12. Guo Yunshen's chart of transformations

tice, the dispersed qi is concentrated at the navel and all parts of the body are coordinated. This is called Little Heaven.

"The next stage is concealed energy. It is free, relaxed, soft, and natural. However, do not be misled by the word soft. It is not soft like grass; rather, it is elastic. This stage deals with changing qi into spirit and concomitantly changing the sinews. It is called Big Heaven. In boxing when your right hand goes forward, the left hand pulls back as though it were tearing cotton or drawing a bow. This is done slowly, not abruptly. When your two hands go forward it is like pulling a cart. That is, just as your legs, not your hands, move the cart, it is your legs, not your hands, that impart strength to your boxing. The rear foot holds strength as though you are going to leap off it across a ditch.

"The highest stage grows from the second. It is called mysterious, the result of marrow washing. It is soft and uses no strength. It lets you move more easily because the energy is concentrated. And this energy merges you with emptiness, the Tao in which "Boxing is non-boxing, non-boxing is boxing." The energy derived is different from actual strength. Although the actions taken are the same, the energy stays inside, controlled by the mind. This is the acme of Xingyi—the best of alchemy, boxing, and the Tao.

The highest stage grows from the second. It is called mysterious, the result of marrow washing. It is soft and uses no strength.

"Simultaneously with your advancement through these stages, there occur three changes in your body: change of bones, change of sinews, and washing of the bone marrow. To change the bones means to hold your body like a mountain. When you stand and move, your bones become hard. To change the sinews is to fuse energy into and through all sinews, forming membranes to them and energizing them. To wash and clean the bone marrow is to relax completely and purify and refine the internal organs by using your mind, thus making your body as light as a feather.

"There are three ways of breathing in Xingyi: basic, intermediate, and advanced. In the basic stage of obvious energy, put your tongue on the roof of your mouth, which is half opened, half closed. Breathe naturally through your nose without attention to inhalation and exhalation. The hands and feet coordinate with your breathing to transform sperm into qi. In the intermediate stage of concealed energy, the mouth and tongue are held the same and you breathe through the nose, but now you pay attention to sinking your breath to the navel, thus transforming qi to spirit. The third and highest breathing stage, related to mysterious energy, is reached unconsciously by doing the first two stages. In this stage your spirit is transformed to emptiness and you do not feel that you are breathing: there is no sound, no smell, and everything is empty.

"How is Xingyi used in the three stages? In the first stage it is like a steel chisel, which goes out strongly but falls like a light piece of bamboo. In the second, it starts like an arrow, and falls weightless like the wind. In the highest stage, it follows the wind and chases the moon. An outsider never sees it hit; if he does, it does not belong to this stage. This is Xingyi, the highest level of achievement: The mind is mindless; you do nothing and have done everything. In the emptiness we find our prenatal bodies. But do not be overly concerned about this. If you try too hard, it will elude you. Instead of trying to achieve it, pretend you already have it. This will help your mind. After all, the mind is the embodiment of your actions: therefore, Xingyi is mind boxing.

"In the basic posture (santi) most of the weight is on your rear foot. In Xingyi the weight is never shared equally: this eases movement and avoids the rigidity of double weighting. It lets you distinguish the soft from the hard (yin and yang). Xingyi is uncomplicated because it is natural. We are in harmony with everything. Do not look for miracles. Carry on like a normal person doing ordinary actions, and with perseverance progress will come.

"You may learn Xingyi simply for health. But if you learn it for boxing purposes, it is more difficult. Whoever

> The third and highest breathing stage, related to mysterious energy, is reached unconsciously by doing the first two stages. In this stage your spirit is transformed to emptiness and you do not feel that you are breathing: there is no sound, no smell, and everything is empty.

is proud will lose. Watch the distance between yourself and an antagonist; study his physical characteristics and stance. When you step forward intend to dig into him. Protect your body with your elbows. Be versatile and flexible; do not be afraid of changing your tactics. Do not use strength. Be calm and you will be stable. Cheng Tinghua told me: 'Whenever I fight someone, I look to see how strong, soft, muscular, or tricky he is. I try to discover his weak points. I never stick to one way: long or short or high or low. Assessing your enemy this way, even if you don't defeat him, you will never be defeated'.

"To practice your movements plant nine numbered bamboo sticks as shown in figure (Fig. 3-13). At first make the distance between them great; gradually decrease it until the sticks are barely a shoulder-width apart. Go from one through nine from inside and then reverse the order, gradually increasing your speed. Avoid colliding with the gates. Later arbitrarily move through them without regard to number. This exercise derives from the Ishing and is excellent in that you may regard the posts as opponents to evade and strike. If you do it long enough, it will produce a great change in you." [27]

Be versatile and flexible; do not be afraid of changing your tactics. Do not use strength. Be calm and you will be stable.

46

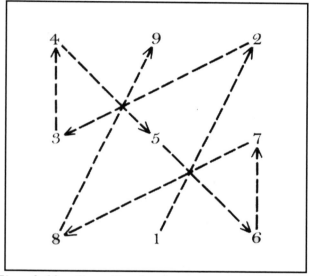

Fig. 3-13. Guo Yunshen's movement diagram

Part II

The Life and Art of Wang Xiangzhai

Note and Caveat

In the first few years of my standing practice with Master Fong Ha, the spirit would often move him, during retreats and other special occasions, to go back to the source. He would pick up Wang Xiangzhai's books, or the books written about Wang Xiangzhai by his students, and proceed to translate portions orally. This was invaluable to us as students. It helped us gain a deeper understanding of both the art and of Wang Xiangzhai's personal life and development.

I was fortunate enough to record some of these sessions on tape and take written notes on others. Imperfect though these may be, the records have been a constant source of inspiration to me in my years of practice. Therefore, I want to share them with my fellow enthusiasts in the chapters that follow. Biographical data translated by Master Fong Ha from books and pamphlets by such luminaries as Yao Zongxun, Lee Yin Arn and the Beijing Yiquan Association are the basis for Chapter 4. The sections Fong Ha translated from Wang Xiangzhai's own books, *The True Course of Yiquan* and *Collection of Experiences in Quan*, are the basis for Chapter 5.

Of course, given the inherent shortcomings of spontaneous oral translations, I do not presume to offer this material, especially the selections in Chapter 5, as definitive translations. Rather, I present them as introductory glimpses into Wang Xiangzhai's genius. Indeed, it is my sincere hope and desire that the very inadequacy of these translated segments will motivate someone somewhere to publish a serious "considered" English translation of

Wang Xiangzhai's collected works. Perhaps one of the many existing Yiquan Organizations, such as the Yiquan Associations of Hong Kong or Beijing, will see fit to commission the undertaking of such a project. It would be an incalculable service to the world-wide community of martial artists in general and Yiquan artists in particular.

Regrettably, also as a result of the nature of the documentation, it is not possible to provide the page numbers for the selections and quotes. In these cases, only the book source of each selection is indicated. In Chapter 4, this will be in the endnotes. In chapter 5 this will be indicated at the end of each selection, abbreviated and in parenthesss: (TTYQ) indicates that the selection comes from *The True Course of Yiquan*; (CEIQ) indicates the selection is from the *Collection of Experiences in Quan*. The additional material quoted from Wang Xuanjie's interview with Wang Xiangzhai, entitled "Essence of Boxing Art" and published in his book *Dachengquan*, (Hong Kong: Hai Feng Publishing Co., Ltd., 1988) will be indicated by (DCQ, p _)

Chapter 4

The Life of Wang Xiangzhai

In the history of Chinese martial arts, the name Wang Xiangzhai stands out as one of the great twentieth-century Chinese geniuses who redefined the nature and possibilities of the art. A poet and formidable martial artist, his life's major accomplishment consisted of re-interpreting, from a twentieth-century perspective, the strict martial arts training he received in his youth from his uncle. Based upon the extensive historical research he conducted throughout his life, Wang Xiangzhai redefined the roots and essence of his art with poetic elegance and scientific simplicity.

Fig. 4-1. Wang Xiangzhai (1)

Wang Xiangzhai's conceptual and developmental breakthroughs led him to a revolutionary redefinition of the conventional relationship of stillness to movement in the martial arts by making stillness primary and movement secondary. He rejected the traditional patterned sequences of movement as the primary method of training. Reaching back to historical roots of Chinese Buddhism and Vedic India, he advocated the practice of stillness and the cultivation of mind and intent as the primary practice.

As we will see, this was not mere empty and pretty theorizing. Wang Xiangzhai's martial capabilities and reputation were proof that his theories were correct. In his heyday, Wang Xiangzhai took on and beat all challengers.

1. The Apprenticeship

Wang Xiangzhai was born in 1885 in the Shenxian district of Hebei province. He was given the name of Ni Libao, was later named Yuseng, and yet later in life adopted the name Wang Xiangzhai.[1] As a small boy, Wang Xiangzhai developed a severe case of asthma which stunted his growth and left him in poor health. When he was 8 years old, in order to remedy his illness and help him regain his health and strength, his father made him take up the practice of Xingyiquan with his Elder Uncle, the famous Guo Yunshen in the neighboring village of Majong.

When he was 8 years old, in order to remedy his illness and help him regain his health and strength, his father made Wang Xiangzhai take up the practice of Xingyiquan with his Elder Uncle, the famous Guo Yunseng

Actually, the old Master did not really want to take on young Wang Xiangzhai as his apprentice, because he was old and suffered from "sickness in the legs" such that he could barely walk. But two things changed his mind. First, his own son and heir to the lineage had an accident; he fell from a horse and died. Also, Wang Xiangzhai had come with excellent recommendations from another relative. Thus, Guo Yunshen relented and agreed to accept Wang Xiangzhai as his live-in student.[2]

It was not long before a profound rapport developed between the two. Young Wang Xiangzhai was highly intelligent in his perception and very diligent in his

Chapter 4 The Life of Wang Xiangzhai

practice. This earned him the respect and affection of his Elder Uncle who recognized in his nephew the qualities necessary for him to become a worthy successor in the lineage of transmission of his Art. As Wang Xiangzhai expressed it later in life, his uncle felt that "if the student is not the right person, he cannot learn and the right person cannot teach him. In other words, progress requires the right combination of student, teacher and Art."[3]

But in his nephew Guo found the right student. Thus, as Wang Xiangzhai later wrote himself, his uncle "...from time to time, would show me his specialties and advised me to show his Art great respect and not follow the habits of my peers."[4] The "habits of my peers" Wang Xiangzhai is talking about refers to the preoccupation of martial artists with the superficial intricacies of form, as opposed to the deep simplicity of essence. Again in Wang Xiangzhai's own words: "When Mr. Guo taught Xingyiquan, the fundamental practice was zhanzhuang, or standing meditation. This was the essence of his teaching."[5]

Young Wang Xiangzhai took his uncle's teachings seriously and within a few years of study and practice he had not only regained his health, but also understood and internalized Xingyiquan's essence.

The reader may recall that this technique of standing Zen meditation, the historical basis and essence of Xingyiquan, was developed to new heights of achievement by Guo Yunshen during his prison years, when he was shackled and forcibly immobilized. Young Wang Xiangzhai took his uncle's teachings seriously and within a few years of study and practice he had not only regained his health, but also understood and internalized Xingyiquan's essence. Thus he developed into a formidable boxer while still only in his teens.

THE TAO OF YIQUAN

It must have been a source of bittersweet pride for Guo Yunshen to see his nephew growing and maturing in the art even as his own advancing age increasingly began to take its toll on him. Already in his mid-seventies, he soon no longer had the strength to even stand up while practicing tui shou, or pushing hands, with Wang Xiangzhai. Yet nothing was allowed to intervene in the transmission of the art and they continued their pushing practice with Kuo sitting "on the northern bed," a term denoting a little brick bench that was part of the hearth in which Wang Xiangzhai always kept a fire going to keep his teacher warm and comfortable.[6]

An extraordinary closeness developed between the two, and Kuo continued to instruct Wang Xiangzhai verbally until his dying day.

As Guo's health continued to decline over the next five to six years, Wang Xiangzhai began to take care of his Uncle day and night as if he were his own son, always being there when needed. Thus an extraordinary closeness developed between the two, and Kuo continued to instruct Wang Xiangzhai verbally until his dying day. Finally, when the time came in 1898, Master Guo reportedly said on his deathbed that among his many disciples, Wang Xiangzhai was the only one who could inherit his legacy and carry it forward.[7]

The skeptic might argue that after only five years of training as a child, and being only 13 years old, Wang Xiangzhai could hardly have progressed enough to have gotten so good as to be able to merit the distinction of inheriting the lineage of transmission. But old Master Guo Yunshen recognized the innate genius and self-discipline of Wang Xiangzhai. He was confident that the rigorous training he exacted of him would in time produce the desired results and make him a worthy successor to the secrets of his art.

Chapter 4 The Life of Wang Xiangzhai

Just how demanding he was of Wang Xiangzhai in his training is illustrated in this story. The first thing young Wang Xiangzhai was to do upon getting up in the morning was to practice his zhanzhuang standing meditation. When Guo Yunshen would get up later, the first thing he would do was to examine the mark of dampness around the place where Wang Xiangzhai was standing. If the floor was not sufficiently wet from perspiration, Wang Xiangzhai would have to stand again until the old Master was satisfied that the floor was wet enough.[8]

2. Early 1900s: The Quest

After the death of Guo Yunshen, young Wang Xiangzhai moved back into his parents' house for a few years. Several incidents during this time proved that he had indeed developed considerable martial arts skill. Once, in 1901 when he was 16 years old, Wang Xiangzhai accompanied his father to Yunyuang village for additional training and practice. On the road, they were ambushed by a group of more then ten bandits, most of them armed, who tried to rob them. But empty-handed as they were, Wang Xiangzhai and his father defeated the whole bunch, causing them to flee in utter terror and amazement. When he would recount the story later on, Wang Xiangzhai's father would always recount with paternal pride the exclamation of one of the fleeing robbers that "this boy is really powerful."[9]

In another incident when he was accompanying his father to another village, he observed two young monks practicing in the great hall of a Buddhist temple. They seemed very advanced in their development to Wang Xiangzhai because of the way they walked, almost skat-

When he was 16 years old, Wang Xiangzhai and his father... were ambushed by a group of more than ten bandits, most of them armed. But empty-handed as they were, Wang Xiangzhai and his father defeated the whole bunch, causing them to flee in utter terror and amazement.

ing-like, with curious long steps, each one leaving the ground for almost ten feet before touching down again. Naturally, he wanted to test skills with them and invited them to do so. They accepted the offer and engaged in several bouts. But to the monks' surprise, and probably even his own, every time Wang Xiangzhai made contact with them, the monks wound up sprawling on the floor. These two incidents and others boosted young Wang Xiangzhai's morale immensely for, having tested his skills, he knew that he had developed something very special.[10]

In 1907 when he was 22 years old, Wang Xiangzhai left his parents' home and village under disharmonious circumstances. He had been befriended by a young relative with whom he had gotten into the bad habit of gambling. Disliking the punishment his mother meted out to him, he and his relative ran away to Beijing to make a living.[11] In Beijing, Wang Xiangzhai joined the army as a cook's helper with the job of cutting wood and carrying water. Once, as he was carrying water, a soldier, not knowing Wang Xiangzhai's martial arts abilities, tried to trip him, but instead, wound up on the ground himself, amazing the rest of the soldiers.

When the captain in charge heard about the incident, he summoned Wang Xiangzhai for an explanation. Wang Xiangzhai explained that he had studied Xingyiquan with the famed Guo Yunshen. This pleased the captain, himself a martial arts champion, so much that he gave Wang Xiangzhai his daughter as his wife and gave him a new job as martial arts instructor to the soldiers.[12] With his improved position, Wang Xiangzhai had the time to improve

Chapter 4   The Life of Wang Xiangzhai

his education and study things besides the martial arts. He turned out to be equally gifted in poetry and calligraphy as in the martial arts. His wife was also an avid martial arts practitioner, and studying Xingyiquan with her husband, also became highly skilled in the art. She also gave birth to their three children, two girls and a boy. The second daughter, Wang Yufong, is still alive today, teaching her father's art of zhanzhuang, standing meditation, in Beijing.

The classics always claim that if studied in their true essence, the practice of the martial arts will result in the refinement of one's personality and character. As illustrated in the following story, this was certainly the case with Wang Xiangzhai, who always was a perfect gentleman and paid the proper respect in dealing with his peers and elders. In 1913, when he was 28 and his reputation as a martial artist already well established in Beijing, a prominent politician invited Wang Xiangzhai to a banquet that also would be attended by the prominent martial arts instructor Mr. Li Ruidong.[13]

When Mr. Li Ruidong arrived, Wang Xiangzhai went over to meet him and introduce himself. When they shook hands, it appeared to all around as if they were just greeting each other, but in reality they were testing each other's inner strength. It turned out Mr. Li could not match Wang Xiangzhai inner strength. His leg became soft and buckled, causing him to have to kneel down. Wang Xiangzhai, observing this, immediately relented and pulled him up, thus saving him from embarrassment and loss of face. Smiling in appreciation, the older gentleman simply turned and left.[14]

The audience was highly disappointed and surprised at this behavior and pressed Wang Xiangzhai for an explanation, asking, "This guy who came to visit you is a very big name in the martial arts. Nobody can compete with him. Why would he just touch you and leave laughing without doing anything?" In reply, Wang Xiangzhai said, "For those who have self-realized as martial artists, when they just touch they know each other's skill and ability. If you really know, there is no need to fight it out."[15]

In 1918 when Wang was 33 years old he ... took the opportunity to embark on a ten-year quest throughout China to seek out other renowned masters to broaden his martial arts horizons.

In 1918 when Wang was 33 years old he had to stop his teaching in Beijing on account of the political climate there. He took the opportunity to embark on a ten-year quest throughout China to seek out other renowned masters to broaden his martial arts horizons.[16] Testing and being tested, he left his footprints in many places both north and south of the great Yangtze River. His encounters during this time of exploration with the representative masters of many different martial arts systems greatly enhanced his field of experience, enabling him to obtain insight into their methods and principles. In this process of enriching his knowledge of the spectrum of traditional Chinese martial arts, Wang Xiangzhai was laying the foundation for his own unique synthesis of them that would bring him great fame in future years.

3. Shaolin Monastery

Of great importance to Wang Xiangzhai's further development was his stay with the monks at the Shaolin Monastery and Temple in Hunan. Here he met Monk Henglin, an outstanding boxer of the Shaolin School. Henglin was large in stature and famous for his strength

Chapter 4 The Life of Wang Xiangzhai

and power. In contrast to him Wang Xiangzhai was thin and looked fragile and unimpressive in appearance. However, the large monk found out that appearances can be misleading, for Wang Xiangzhai could discharge a tremendously explosive power from his small body within a split second. This earned him the respect of the huge monk and the two became very good friends during Wang Xiangzhai's stay at the monastery. They incessantly exchanged views and learned much from each other through discussions and competitions.[17]

Monk Henglin's superior, Abbot Benhong, also known as Benjiao, also took kindly to Wang Xiangzhai. Despite his advanced age of 90 years, Abbot Benhong imparted a lot of valu-

Fig. 4-2. Shaolin Monastery

able boxing theory to young Wang Xiangzhai, from which he received immeasurable benefit.[18] As a matter of fact, Wang Xiangzhai's purpose in coming to the monastery had been precisely to investigate the nature and principles of the Xinyiquan boxing art practiced there. Thus Wang Xiangzhai learned that Xinyiquan (Heart/Mind and Intent Boxing) and Xingyiquan (Form and Intent Boxing) came from the same historical source, and he learned to appreciate their similarities as well as differences. After several months' stay at the Shaolin Temple, Wang Xiangzhai bade good-bye to his friend Henglin and Abbot Benhong and once more started on his road in quest of adventure and truth.

Next, Wang Xiangzhai went to Hunan where he met the great Xinyiquan Grandmaster, Jie Tiefu. Mr. Jie was over 50 years old at the time and considered to be quite an eccentric because he never talked to anyone about his art, and for that matter, never talked much to anyone about anything. Wang Xiangzhai requested a match and Mr. Jie Tiefu obliged. They fought ten rounds and Wang Xiangzhai was defeated soundly all ten rounds. He had finally met his match. But, not wanting to give up yet, Wang Xiangzhai then asked, "Can I match you in weapons?" At this Mr. Jie Tiefu laughed and said, "Weapons are nothing more than extensions of the human hand. If I can defeat you with my hands, I can defeat you with weapons." But again, he obliged Wang Xiangzhai, and they fought another ten rounds with weapons. Again, as Mr. Jie Tiefu predicted, Wang Xiangzhai was soundly defeated all ten rounds.[19]

Wang Xiangzhai requested a match and Mr. Jie Tiefu obliged. They fought ten rounds and Wang Xiangzhai was defeated soundly all ten rounds.

After that, humbled and embarrassed, Wang Xiangzhai made ready to pack his bags and leave. Seeing this, the eccentric Mr. Jie Tiefu said, "You want to come back in three years? Is that what you want? I'm old now and don't have that many years left. You might as well stay a little longer. Don't be embarrassed because I have a lot of experience. Throughout my life I have met a lot of good accomplished people, but I haven't met anyone as good as you are. Now, why don't you stay and let us make friends." At that invitation, Wang Xiangzhai paid his respects and stayed with Mr. Jie Tiefu for over a year, and during that time made enormous progress. When the time came to say good-bye, Mr. Jie Tiefu accompanied Wang Xiangzhai to the border and left him with these words, "As far as your accomplishments south of the river are concerned, I dare not say, but north of the river I don't think anyone can hurt you." They bade farewell with tears in their eyes.[20]

Wang Xiangzhai then crossed the Yangtze River into southern China where again he encountered and engaged numerous martial arts specialists in discussion and competition. Among those he engaged in successful contests were Mr. Fang Shizhang in Zhejiang Province, who was famed for his devastating mastery of Wujiliaoshou (five-hand striking skills), and Mr. Liu Peixian from Xi'an, who had mysterious leg attack skills.[21]

Wang Xiangzhai then paid his respects and stayed with Mr. Jie Tiefu for over a year, and during that time made enormous progress.

4. Wang Xiangzhai and Dunhuang

Wang Xiangzhai continued his travels in northern China through the mid-1920s, seeking always a closer examination of the Buddhist origins and essence of the martial arts and attempting to incorporate that essence into the grand synthesis that was beginning to emerge in his practice and thinking. Of crucial importance to this search were two events.

The first was the discovery, made in the process of excavating caves at Dunhuang, of Buddhist texts, paintings, and statuary dating back to the Tang Dynasty circa 750 C.E. This was material, then, that preceded the great outpouring of writings related to Buddhist spiritual and martial arts which occurred over the next five centuries. It gave access, finally, to earlier, purer, unadulterated forms.

That the context for these discoveries was religious is not surprising.

The many internal turmoils in Chinese history have meant that there was never any common and consistent source recording its civil and military history, nor the Indian contributions to it. The continuity we do find is that documented within religious groups, particularly Buddhism. Monastic records contain accounts of many practices and events. Particularly in the transmission of the health and martial arts, the statuary and painting arts of the monasteries and temples have played an essential role.

Fig. 4-3. Dunhuang Cave murals depicting martial stances

Statuary and painting arts give a visible record of the aspect of Buddhist practice that recognizes no dichotomy between movement and stillness in either body or mind. It is this statuary that traces the earliest Quanfa positions and gestures so clearly that they can be recognized today. For example, the "Protectors of the Doctrine" that often flank entrance door of altars in temples and shrines are frequently depicted as two Vajra kings in the classical defense stances of Quanfa. Their forearms are often held in the traditional protective positions while performing tactically significant mudras or ritualized gestures with their hands.[22] Not many people realize that the praying position we are so familiar with in the West, with hands joined before the chest, is an ancient Vajramukti-based defensive position.

Chapter 4 The Life of Wang Xiangzhai

According to Wang Xuanjie, within Wang Xiangzhai's tradition, Xingyiquan itself was preserved and transmitted by way of temple art. "A Shanxi native Ji Jike of Ming Dynasty (1386-1644) dis-covered Illustrated Yueh Fei's Boxing Manual on the wall of a broken temple on Zhongnan Hill. Ji was a warrior himself. When he got the manual, he studied and practiced it diligently, and thus lay the foundations for Xingyiquan of the later times." [23]

Fig. 4-4. Dunhuang statuary depicting martial stances

Within this context, the importance of the discoveries at the Dunhuang caves cannot be overestimated. Some Dunhuang cave statues represent the Bodhisattva and guardians who are in the on-guard positions of Quanfa. Other wall paintings show many deities and arhats in Quanfa positions and stances. For example, Cave #290 features wrestling scenes, cave #195 contains "paired exercises," cave #249 portrays "Hercules Holding Show," and cave #61 depicts scenes of swordmanship.[24]

The creation/transmission of the Xingyiquan system through temple art became a precedent for the reconstruction of Xingyiquan that Wang Xiangzhai himself under-took after gaining knowledge of the Dunhuang statues and paintings. In 1926, the second event of crucial importance in this regard occurred when he met the reclusive Xinyi Master Huang Muqiao.

Wang Xiangzhai recounted the impact Huang Muqiao made on him in the first draft (1942) of his first book, *The True Course of Yiquan.* "In the Sui and Tang Dynasties (581-907 C.E..), a certain "Health Dance" was very popular at the time. Both scholars and martial artists practiced the art for general health maintenance and martial arts training. Later on that art was lost. Among the contemporary martial artists of our time, Mr. Huang Muqiao has been very active in gathering and interpreting the "Health Dance" from the wall pictures at the archeological site of Dunhuang. Thus he was able to reconstruct the techniques and recover the shen (spirit) of the ancient "Health Dance."[25]

"I learned the "Health Dance" from Mr. Huang Muqiao, and thus I also came to understand its essence. I dare not keep it a secret, and therefore transmit it to those who study with me".

"During the time of the North Crusades (before the communists), I met Mr. Huang Muqiao and I learned the Health Dance from him, and came to understand its essence. I dare not keep it a secret, and therefore transmit it to those who study with me. But among all my students, there are only about ten who have really mastered it."[26]

In celebration of his learning the ancient "Health Dance," Wang Xiangzhai wrote the following poem:

The body moves like a dance of waves
Like the flowing dragon and the white crane in play
Like the twisting of the frightened snake
The intent and strength move
As if sailing on the waves[28]

Contemporary experts in Dunhuang art and history point to the western wall of Cave #272 built during the Northern Liang period (421-442 C.E.), apparently depicting a series of qigong or martial arts postures, as one of the

Chapter 4 The Life of Wang Xiangzhai

Fig. 4-5. Dunhuang cave #272

most likely candidates for Wang Huang Muqiao's inspirational reconstruction.[27]

Learning the "Health Dance" provided Wang Xiangzhai with the missing link in his search for historical roots and the creation of his own system. It is significant to note that the Sui Dynasty came to power only twenty years after the death of Bodhidharma. Recognizing that the essence of the ancient "Health Dance" was contemporary with, and identical to, the essence of Bodhidharma's teachings on changing the muscles, ligaments and tendons (Yijinjing) and washing the bone marrow (Shi Soei Chin), Wang Xiangzhai was convinced he had found the direct historical and essential link he had been searching for.

5. Naming the Art

The essence Wang Xiangzhai had found was the use of Yi, usually translated as mind or intention, in the cultivation and training of the body for health and martial arts purposes. Wang Xiangzhai wrote that Bodhidharma "combined the five animal frolics, created in the Han Dynasty (206 B.C.E. -220 C.E.) by Hua Tou, the 'first Chinese Doctor,' with the methods for changing the ligaments (Yijinjing) and washing the bone marrow (Shi Soei Chin) to create the system of Yiquan," mind or intention boxing. In deference to Bodhidharma and Buddhist historical tradition, Wang Xiangzhai called the system he created Yiquan.[29]

Xinyiquan, Xingyiquan and Liuhebu are collectively referred to as the school of Zhongnan Hill Boxing.

To further clarify Wang Xiangzhai's historical derivation, it must be noted that the Xingyiquan (Form-Intent Boxing) Wang Xiangzhai had been trained in was originally known in Hebei Province as Xinyiquan (Heart-Intent Boxing), while in Henan province it was known as Liuhebu (six directions steps). Wang Xiangzhai explained this as follows: "When tracing the origin of Mr. Li Laidong of Henan, you will see that he was the great-grandson of Mr. Li Zhihe who was the teacher of Dai Longbang. The Yuans of Ji Yuan County named the boxing differently (Liuhebu), but it is in fact the same school with Mr. Li as its founder. By changing Xin Yi (heart-intention) into Xing Yi (Form-intention), Mr. Dai did not betray the original meaning of Xin Yi, because boxing originated from Liu Fa (six ways)."

Although three different strains of the art developed, they were historically and essentially identical, differing only in outward form. Referring to the ancient temple manual of Zhongnan Hill upon which they were based, Xinyiquan, Xingyiquan and Liuhebu were collectively referred to as the school of Zhongnan Hill Boxing.[30]

In his own synthesis, seeking both to unify and to distill both systems to their historical roots and essence, Wang Xiangzhai eliminated both the words Xin (heart-mind) and Xing (form), simply and purely calling it Yiquan, thereby emphasizing the supreme importance of the intentional component of the Mind. What Wang Xiangzhai was attempting to accomplish with this was to remedy a situation that he found highly objectionable— namely, the obsession many of his students, as well as martial artists in general, had with the intricate forms and patterns which constituted the practice of almost all martial arts.

Fig. 4-6. Wang Xiangzhai (2)

Wang Xiangzhai felt they were putting the cart before the horse, in that such obsession with outward form became an insurmountable barrier to the discovery and cultivation of inner essence. This inner essence, he believed, could only be grasped and developed by the mind. Only the proper training of the mind, he argued, would allow the body to rediscover its innate ability for natural movement and thereby develop the capacity to react spontaneously and appropriately to any given situation. Thus Wang Xiangzhai eliminated the Xing or forms from Xingyiquan to create the system of no-form, only Mind: Yiquan.

6. The 1930s: Domestic & Foreign Challenges

After learning the ancient "Health Dance," Wang Xiangzhai again ventured forth and began actively propagating and teaching Yiquan and its tenets everywhere he went. In particular, he stayed for quite a while in Shanghai, where there lived a great number of the country's best martial artists. The better known students of Wang Xiangzhai's Shanghai period included Han Xingqiao and Han Xingyuan, Yu Pengxi, Wang Shuehe, Mu Jianzhao, Gao Zhendong, Zhu Guolu, Zhu Guozhen, Bu Enfu, Zhang Changxin and Zhang Changyi.

An unending stream of domestic and, increasingly, of foreign martial artists came to Wang Xiangzhai's door asking for a challenge bout in the hope of besting the Master. None succeeded.

In Shanghai, an unending stream of domestic and, increasingly, of foreign martial artists came to Wang Xiangzhai's door asking for a challenge bout in the hope of besting the Master. None succeeded. One by one, Wang Xiangzhai successfully and oftentimes unceremoniously, put his opponents in their place—usually on the floor—always emerging the undisputed victor.

Among foreign challengers there were several high-caliber European boxers as well as several high-ranking Japanese martial artists. While in Shanghai, Wang Xiangzhai met the Director of Boxing of the European YMCA, who arranged a bout with the then World Featherweight Champion, a Hungarian by the name of Inge, who was visiting in Shanghai. When the two had their encounter, the Hungarian champion tried to knock Wang Xiangzhai out with a straight punch. But Wang Xiangzhai, with no more than a barely visible shiver of his left hand, threw the champion on the floor. After his defeat, Mr. Inge wrote an article in the London Times detailing his understanding of the Chinese martial arts. In general he spoke

Fig. 4-7. Wang Xiangzhai (far right) with other martial arts luminaries, including Zhang Zhaodong in the center

very highly of the development of the Chinese martial arts, and in particular stressed the great respect he had for Wang Xiangzhai's accomplishment.[31]

After that, in 1939, Wang Xiangzhai had a bout with a very famous Japanese martial artist, Kenichi Sawei, who was a fifth dan in Judo and ninth dan in Kenpo. Again, the challenger was defeated decisively. Each time, the moment they made contact, Wang Xiangzhai bounced him off effortlesly. The Japanese was so impressed that he decided to stay, and he studied with Wang Xiangzhai for almost twelve years. After completion of his studies with Wang Xiangzhai, Mr. Sawei returned to Japan and began to teach the essence of Wang Xiangzhai's Yiquan system, embellished with his own variations. Mr. Sawei called his system TaiKi-Ken. In his book *TaiKi-Ken*, Mr. Sawei gave his own personal account of his encounters with Wang Xiangzhai:

Fig. 4-8. Kenichi Sawai

Since at that time I was a fifth dan in Judo, I had a degree of confidence in my abilities in combat techniques. When I had my first opportunity to try myself in a match with Wang Xiangzhai, I gripped his right hand and tried to use a technique. But I at once found myself being hurled through the air. I saw the uselessness of surprise and sudden attacks with this man. Next I tried grappling. I gripped his left hand and his right lapel and tried the techniques I knew, thinking that, if the first attack failed, I would be able to move into a grappling technique when we fell. But the moment we came together, Wang Xiangzhai instantaneously gained complete control of my hand and thrust it out and away from himself. No matter how many times I tried to get the better of him, the results were always the same. Each time I was thrown, he tapped me lightly on my chest just over my heart. When he did this, I experienced a strange and frightening pain that was like a heart tremor.

Still I did not give up. I requested that he pit himself against me in fencing. We used sticks instead of swords; and, even though the stick he used was short, he successfully parried all my attacks and prevented my making a single point. At the end of the match he said quietly, "The sword—or the staff—both are extensions of the hand."

This experience robbed me of all confidence in my own abilities. My outlook, I thought, would be very dark indeed, unless I managed to obtain instruction from Wang Xiangzhai. I did succeed in studying with him; and, acting on his advice, I instituted a daily course in Zen training. Gradually I began to feel as if I had gained a little bit of the expansive Chinese martial spirit.[32]

Chapter 4 The Life of Wang Xiangzhai

7. The 1940s: Beijing and Dachengquan

In 1937 Wang Xiangzhai was persuaded by friends to return to Beijing to make his home there and establish a martial arts training center. As part of his program to propagate Yiquan, he wrote a series of articles and gave a series of interviews that were published in the Beijing newspaper *Shibao* (*Truth Daily*). In these sometimes quite polemical writings and no-holds-barred interviews, Wang Xiangzhai expressed his observations and criticisms concerning Chinese martial arts. At the same time, he delineated how the theory and practice of his own system of Yiquan corrected the inadequacies he perceived in the traditional methods of Chinese health and martial arts training.

In these sometimes quite polemical writings and no-holds-barred interviews, Wang Xiangzhai expressed his observations and criticisms concerning Chinese martial arts.

Fig. 4-9. Wang Xiangzhai with fellow martial artists

The thrust of his critical arguments against traditional theory and practice was twofold. The first, alluded to previously, was the obsessive preoccupation with forms and patterns of movement on the parts of the adherents of traditional martial arts. The rote learning of such traditional practice routines, he argued, actually prevents students from penetrating to the essence of martial art ability. This essence, as he defined it, consists of the body's innate and natural ability to respond spontaneously and appropriately to the demands of any given situation.

Such response can be developed only by training the Yi (mind or intention) to such an extent that it achieves complete mastery over one's Qi (vital force). And this can only be accomplished in the stillness of zhanzhuang, his method of formless standing meditation, never in the movement of traditional structured forms. Wang Xiangzhai taught that the acme of martial arts ability lies in the paradox that only the movement (of Qi, or energy) cultivated in stillness can produce stillness (of mind) in physical movement.

> **The rote learning of such traditional practice routines, Wang Xiangzhai argued, actually prevents students from penetrating to the essence of martial art ability.**

The second major impediment to a true renaissance of the martial arts in China, Wang Xiangzhai argued, was the traditional method of transmission. In particular, he issued a blistering critique of the traditional aspects of secrecy and selectivity in transmission, as well as of the traditional authoritarian teacher-student relationship. Wang Xiangzhai noted that secrecy and selectivity in transmission lead to excessive and neurotic competition and thereby to lack of cooperative research between differing schools of martial arts. He therefore regarded these practices of the hoarding of secrets and their carefully selected transmission by the Master to one or two students, usually in the family lineage, as one of the main

Chapter 4 The Life of Wang Xiangzhai

contributing factors in the decline and impoverishment of the Chinese martial arts. As he wrote in his first preface to *The True Course of Yiquan*:

"If people have these kinds of thoughts of secrecy, there is no more fortune left in mankind. That is why in our country, we have so many weaklings and we cannot compare with the other countries because of this sickness that exists. In other words, knowledge should not be kept a secret because it belongs to all mankind. Knowledge does not belong to any one country or nation or group, because all knowledge exists under the sun, and anything under the sun cannot be kept a secret. I take up to teach martial arts as a profession. I have never refused anyone who came to study with me. Anyone, who has a desire to learn, I will teach. What I teach, I will teach with all my might. Whenever asked, I will answer, and I will answer to the fullest."[33]

As to the other target of his criticism, the traditional authoritarian master-disciple relationship, Wang Xiangzhai was no less scathing in his indictment. Like the secrecy issue, he pinpointed it as one of the major contributing factors to the sorry state of affairs he perceived in the decline of the martial arts. "This awful, ugly tradition", he wrote, "produces basically masters and slaves." It sets up a neurotic competitive dynamic between students of differing systems that "my teacher is better than yours, yours is not as good as mine," while at the same time creating an exploitative relationship between teacher and student. Therefore, Wang Xiangzhai wrote:

"If we continue with this kind of system, the Way (Tao)

> Knowledge should not be kept a secret because it belongs to all mankind. Knowledge does not belong to any one country or nation or group, because all knowledge exists under the sun, and anything under the sun cannot be kept a secret.

of Martial Arts will never become great. It is only when someone has something to teach and someone wants to learn, that the proper situation for teaching exists. Kow-towing 3000 times and calling the teacher "Great Sifu" does not make him a teacher, nor does it make the student a student, for that has really nothing to do with what you're teaching. Knowledge is the most sacred thing in the universe. That is the reason I so forcefully emphasize breaking down the master-disciple relationship."[34]

It is understandable that Wang Xiangzhai's writings became extremely controversial. On the one hand, they were welcomed with great enthusiasm by the devotees of Yiquan. On the other hand, they were perceived by many members of the greater martial arts community as an insult to their traditions. This was only to be expected of course, for like in any other field of knowledge, a great discovery cannot avoid conflict with the forces of conservatism and tradition. To add fuel to the fire, Wang Xiangzhai issued a standing invitation in the newspaper to all martial artists to come and join him in discussions and/or competition, setting aside every Sunday afternoon for this purpose. Predictably, he was taken up on his offer by numerous practitioners from every conceivable martial arts discipline, and an unending stream of contestants knocked on Mr. Wang Xiangzhai's door to investigate the principles of Yiquan and experience the truth of it at the hands of the Master.

Wang Xiangzhai issued a standing invitation in the newspaper to all martial artists to come and join him in discussions and/or competition, setting aside every Sunday afternoon for this purpose.

One of these is worth recounting, as it shows the extraordinary degree of control Wang Xiangzhai had developed in his art. There was a very prominent Xingyiquan Master by the name of Hong Lianshun who was very big and strong. His famous act was to take a little

76

Chapter 4 The Life of Wang Xiangzhai

brick from the Great Wall and smash it to powder using only a single palm. Wang Xiangzhai accepted his challenge with a smile, and when Hong Lianshun, using all his power, tried to chop Wang Xiangzhai, he merely raised his arm, and discharging only slightly, threw Hong Lianshun just so that he landed on the sofa. Hong Lianshun couldn't believe what happened, so Wang Xiangzhai said, "Come

Fig. 4-10. Wang Xiangzhai with Beijing group

up and try it again, this time I will have you sit down in the same place again." Hong Lianshun tried several more times, but no matter how hard he tried to evade and not land back on the sofa, every time he wound up sitting back on the sofa. He later told someone "I tried to land any place except the sofa, but Wang Xiangzhai lifted his hand, went to the right and left, and, when he found the right place, discharged and again I fell on the sofa." Only one time did Wang Xiangzhai misjudge slightly. He discharged using a little bit too much energy, and threw

Hung on the sofa with so much force that its wooden frame shattered.[35]

Mr. Hong Lianshun, being a man of great integrity, was shamed by his defeats. Immediately he humbled himself and requested instruction from Wang Xiangzhai. They talked for a long period of time, and as Wang Xiangzhai explained to him the principles and theory of Yiquan, Mr. Hung was enlightened as to its superiority. He then brought all his own students to study with Wang Xiangzhai.[36]

"Knowledge really has no end. How then can we call it "Great Accomplishment"? There is no finishing point.

In this and subsequent encounters Wang Xiangzhai defeated all comers. As a result, his fame and that of Yiquan began to assume such legendary proportions that the more zealous of his followers, following the lead of a newspaper editor who first coined the phrase, began calling Wang Xiangzhai's system Dachengquan, meaning "Great Achievement Boxing." At first, Wang Xiangzhai felt he could not decline the honor his followers bestowed on him with this change of name. He wrote, "After they tried the practice of Yiquan, my friends and students found it as sweet as honey and were overjoyed. That is why they gave me the two words Dacheng (Great Achievement) to name my system. At the time I felt I could not decline their respect and therefore allowed it to be called that way."

But later on Wang Xiangzhai had second thoughts about the matter. In his own words: "Knowledge really has no end. How then can we call it "Great Accomplishment"? There is no finishing point."[37] That is why he did not want to continue with the name Dachengquan and went back to calling his system Yiquan. But once again,

Chapter 4 The Life of Wang Xiangzhai

a custom proved to be more readily introduced than eradicated. In defiance of the founder's wishes, many of the System's practitioners, especially in Beijing, even today, continue to refer to Wang Xiangzhai system as Dachengquan.

After the Communists came to power in 1949, Wang Xiangzhai was forced to abandon the Yiquan Club he had established in the Ancestral Temple in Beijing. He was prohibited from teaching the mar-tial aspects of his system and lim-ited to teaching only its health as-pects, or zhanzhuang standing meditation, in the Zhong Shan Gar-den. In 1950, he was briefly ap-pointed to serve in the China Ath-letic Association, but due to con-flicts with the new regime, his ten-ure there did not last long and he resigned his position after a very brief period of service.[38] In 1951, Wang Xiangzhai was invited to teach the zhanzhuang standing meditation practice for health at the Hebei Institute for Traditional Chinese Medicine.

Fig. 4-11. Wang Xiangzhai in later years

Thus, during the final decade of his life, Wang Xiangzhai, being prevented from the teaching of Yiquan as a martial art, devoted himself to conducting research into the connections between Yiquan and traditional Chinese health maintenance practices. In this he was again very successful. At the present time, the standing meditation technique of Yiquan has spread all over China, and a great number of investigations into zhanzhuang have been published in articles and books. The time and effort Wang Xiangzhai spent investigating the health maintenance aspects of his work have blossomed and born countless fruits.

In July of 1963, Wang Xiangzhai died in Tientsin. Growing from the germination of a great dream, this small and humble man had flowered into a truly revolutionary giant in the Chinese culture of healing and martial arts. Indeed, the impeccability of his legacy and the profundity of his insights will continue to fertilize the growth of the healing and martial arts throughout the world for untold centuries to come.

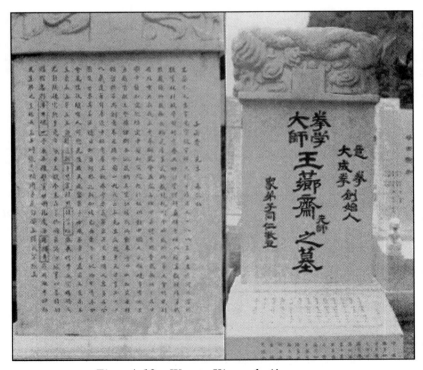

Fig. 4-12. Wang Xiangzhai's grave

Chapter 5
Selected Writings of Wang Xiangzhai

The body moves like a dance of waves
Like the flowing dragon and the white crane in play
Like the twisting of the frightened snake
Intent and strength move as if sailing on the waves

Wang Xiangzhai

1. Introduction

A. Historical origins

"The standing exercise represents a very special accumulation of knowledge in China. But in the past there were very few people who paid attention to it because most people thought it was too simple. They wondered how, by sitting or standing in a single posture without moving, can you improve health? When people wonder this, it is because they do not really understand the essence of standing. In reality, in practicing the exercise of standing without moving, we can not only increase physical strength, but also awaken healing processes within the body, allowing the body to cure itself of all kinds of chronic diseases it might have accumulated during a lifetime. Therefore, in preventative medicine, standing exercises have great value. In fact, it is one of the most appropriate ways of exercising. (CEIQ)

Fig. 5-1. Cover of Wang Xiangzhai's book

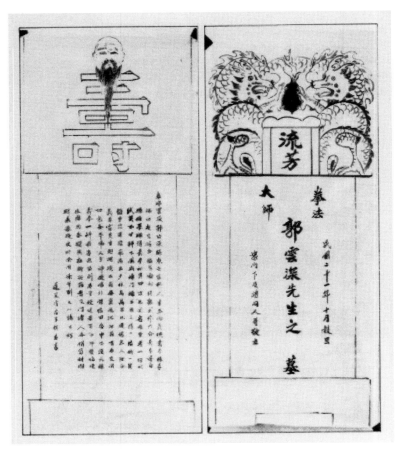

Fig. 5-2. Pages from the manuscripts

Standing can be compared to the work of Zen: First, you start with the precepts, then you cultivate wisdom, then you verify with the mind, and finally you achieve enlightenment in the void.

Standing can be compared to the work of Zen: First, you start with the precepts, then you cultivate wisdom, then you verify with the mind, and finally you achieve enlightenment in the void. Only when we have completed the work of understanding emptiness and the exploration of polarities, can we practice the Tao. So in this respect, the work of Zen and the work of martial arts are the same. (TCYQ)

"During the Han Dynasty, Joa Tou, created the "five animal frolics," which are the substance of the art of standing. But during the period that followed, few people practiced the art, and gradually it was lost until the middle

82

of the Northern Dynasty, when Bodhidharma came to China from India. Bodhidharma taught his disciples the Sutras, but also techniques for strengthening their muscles and ligaments. He combined the "five animal frolics" and the methods for changing the ligaments (Yijinjing) and washing the bone marrow (Shi Soei Ching) to create the Yiquan system (mind or intention boxing), also called Xinyiquan (heart and mind boxing). (TCYQ)

B. Criticism of normal exercise

"In general, most athletic exercises tend to be overactive, and to a certain extent injurious to the body. And most exercise only benefits a certain part of the body. For example, if you lift weight with one hand, you develop muscle only in that one hand and you have a kind of cemented and limited exercise. Therefore, if those who are defective in health do not practice the appropriate exercises, they not only do not regain their health, but they are injured. In more serious cases people may die because they do the wrong exercises.

In general, most athletic exercises tend to be overactive, and to a certain extent injurious to the body. And most exercise only benefits a certain part of the body.

"Exercises should not create abnormal results. In the past, many prominent martial artists spent their entire lives practicing exercises that were opposed to the natural processes of human life. When they grew old they became paralyzed or withered, and this is nothing more than an indication that their exercises were opposed to the normality of life.

"If the exercises are inappropriate, the result will be fatigue, regenerative processes will slow down, the circulation of the blood will not be normal, and health, as a consequence, will be injured.

C. Standing as preferred exercise

"In general, as a person engages in most exercise, the heart rate will quicken and he'll pant when he breathes to the point that he has to stop exercising, so the heart and breathing can normalize. At the end of such exercise the person will experience fatigue. (CEIQ)

"Quan, on the other hand, offers an alternative for stimulating the body. In Quan the ligaments, the flesh (muscles), the bones, the blood, every single cell function in a normal way as opposed to what occurs in the kind of exercises discussed above.

> As the person does Quan exercises, the body will also become fatigued, and won't be able to bear it any longer. Yet the heartbeat will not increase and the breathing will not increase.

"As the person does Quan exercises, the body will also become fatigued, and won't be able to bear it any longer. Yet the heartbeat will not increase and the breathing will not increase. On the contrary, after Quan, breathing will feel much easier than before, and circulation of the blood becomes much more regular than before beginning the Quan. Breathing and circulation will be normal while exercising, and the person will not be affected one way or the other. Therefore, Quan exercising is suitable for persons of all ages and sexes.

"Quan exercise does not demand any type of stance or movement and the nervous system is not stimulated, resulting in nervousness. As a matter of fact, the practitioner becomes relaxed, which is one of the most important effects of Quan, especially compared to the others types of exercising. (CEIQ)

Fig. 5-3. Wang Xiangzhai in Universal Post Posture

2. Zhanzhuang: Pile Standing

A. Unification is simplification

"There were initially many different methods of zhanzhuang, or standing meditation, such as the Taming the Dragon stance, the Taming the Tiger stance, the santi stance, etc. Now we will begin taking away the complications, and derive a very simple method. We will take the essence, the good points of all the systems of standing and combine them into one. We call this the universal stance. This stance is very beneficial for developing energy flow, and, functionally, it is also good for combat. It benefits defense and offense, as well as the opening up of the flow of qi. Most beginners, within a few days of practice, will begin to experience the benefits. However, this cannot be explained in writing, for its wonders are beyond description. (TCYQ)

> **In daily life, the exerciser should, at any place or time, pay attention to body postures in walking, sitting, standing or lying, and regard them as part of proper training.**

"In daily life, the exerciser should, at any place or time, pay attention to body postures in walking, sitting, standing or lying, and regard them as part of proper training. This is done based on zhuangfa or "pile skills"—the skill of keeping steadfast like a pile under all circumstances. One sets all parts of the body to an appropriate state, keeps the body erect, with a mind free from any distractions, regulating the mind and the breath, conserving the muscles, so that the natural energy of the cells can be directed from inside to outside through the whole body. In doing so, the practitioner trains muscles, bones, and nervous system without knowing it. What is crucial here is that one should concentrate the mind on perceiving the delicate motion and stillness inside the body. When such a realm is reached, one will certainly understand the magical effect of pile skills. So zhuangfa is the first thing one should learn to practice. (DCQ, p. 43)

B. Conducting internal investigations

"Posture-wise, we must avoid looking up and tilting the head back, because that breaks the straightness of the neck. Also, do not arch the back. The elbows and the knees should be neither totally straight nor overly bent. The best way is to have them half bent and half straight, that is to say, unlocked; then the ligaments will be stretched. Keep the head straight and also the lower back. Then the qi will be able to sink, and the mind will be quiet and at ease. The tips of the fingers and toes should be slightly extended, the tongue should be touching the palate slightly, and every pore of the body should be slightly open. Practice this way, and your internal energy flow will expand outward easily of its own accord. Your weaknesses will become strengths and you will easily come to self-realization. (TCYQ)

Posture-wise, we must avoid looking up and tilting the head back, because that breaks the straightness of the neck. Also, do not arch the back. The elbows and the knees should be neither totally straight nor overly bent.

"While we're practicing our standing, we investigate the functioning of the joints of the body, as well as the ligaments and muscles, and the double usage of tension and relaxation. Single or double here doesn't mean one hand or two hands or one or two legs. It means that in the head, hands, trunk, shoulders, legs, elbows, knees, pelvis, and all the joints of the body, regardless of how slightly we exert ourselves, we have the sensation that tension and relaxation are all relative to one another. In other words, that relatively speaking, every single joint will have substantiation and insubstantiation, tension and relaxation, and so on.

C. Promoting energy flow through non-exertion

"Those who want to get the benefits from martial arts must begin with the fundamental work of zhanzhuang, or standing meditation, for the purpose of refining the basic human energy flow. The work of zhanzhuang will transform the weak into the strong and turn clumsiness into agility. (TCYQ)

The most important thing is to avoid exerting ourselves either mentally or physically. If we use physical strength, our energy, or qi, will be congested and blocked.

"In the study of the method of standing... the most important thing is to avoid exerting ourselves either mentally or physically. If we use physical strength, our energy, or qi, will be congested and blocked. When our qi is blocked, our intention, or Yi, is stopped. When our intention is blocked, our spirit, or shen, will be distracted. And when our spirit is distracted, we will be deluded into thinking we're making progress while actually we're regressing. (TCYQ)

D. Movement and stillness

"We've been talking here about standing without any movement. The person is not doing anything, but inside the body, every single cell is beginning to work and exercise. The circulation of the blood will begin to function at its maximum capacity, and every function of the body will begin to work in the most normal way; every part of the body inside will work vigorously, while the outward form of the body is inactive. In this way, every part of the body, all organs and every function of the body is speeding up and slowing down in an appropriate manner. The heart will not enlarge, as happens in other types of exercises. In other words, within the body, every part of the body will contribute to normal functioning in an equal manner, compared to the athletic exercises in which the heart is overworked and the breathing responds by also being overworked.

"In standing, everything will work in an equal manner. Therefore we must understand that in the study of Quan, a big movement is not as good as a small movement, and a small movement is not as good as no movement. Not moving outwardly, that is the real movement. (CEIQ)

In the study of Quan, a big movement is not as good as a small movement, and a small movement is not as good as no movement. Not moving outwardly, that is the real movement.

"If you find standing during practice boring, you can move slightly, but you must understand that when you move, you must move as if you cannot stop, and when you want to stop, you must feel as if you cannot stop. That means you should have only the intention of movement, and not the fruit or result of the movement. You should use only your intention, and not emphasize the outward form of the movement. The reason is that once we have the form, the strength is dispersed. Without form the spirit will be centered. When the body is broken, the strength is dispersed, which is why the practice has to be slow. Because when you practice slowly, then all parts of the body, including every single cell, will work in unison. (CEIQ)

E. Polarity as a tool of enlightenment

"Motion and stillness, substantiation and insubstantiation, fast and slow, loose and tight, forward and backward, left and right, up and down, leading and following, receiving and discharging, opening and closing, stretching and contracting, raising and suppressing, lifting and throwing down, swallowing and spitting out, yang and yin, slanting and straight, long and short, big and small, hard and soft, etc, etc: these are the opposites and polarities, the essence of which we must understand. Then, understanding these polarities, we must come back to the beginning to understand what makes them, because these polarities cannot be divided into two opposites. Once you do that, you will never understand what they are. This is the essence of our exercise. (CEIQ)

"Within our exercise, looseness is tightness, tightness is looseness; substantiation is insubstantiation and vice versa. We have to find the appropriate middle ground between substantiation and insubstantiation, and to do that, we must find the root of substantiation and insubstantiation, the essence of all these polarities. (CEIQ)

"If we think of increasing our physical strength, the technique is not to use one's strength, because if one uses one's strength, there is no hope of increase. Also, if one wishes to increase agility, it is better not to move, because when one moves physically, one will have no hope of increasing agility. (CEIQ)

If you master the essence of the changes from substantial to insubstantial and vice versa, then your understanding will be complete and your opponent cannot trace your changes.

"If you master the essence of the changes from substantial to insubstantial and vice versa, then your understanding will be complete and your opponent cannot trace your changes. That is why my teacher Guo Yunshen always said, "Form and intention are not the true things. When your skill, your art, has become totally natural, then the wonders will appear."(TCYQ)

3. Shili: Building Strength

A. Sources of strength

"If you want to investigate the source of your strength, you will find it in expanding your lower back, tucking under your pelvis, lifting up your knee and sinking your qi. Then your whole body is solidly planted in the ground. Thus you stabilize your body by maintaining your center. This will enable you to deal with your opponent by sticking, evading, and following. (TCYQ)

If you want to investigate the source of your strength, you will find it in expanding your lower back, tucking under your pelvis, lifting up your knee and sinking your qi.

"If a person can master the essence of all this in practice, then when he goes out to meet his opponent, he will automatically know what to do. He will be able to change so that no matter how powerful his opponent is, all he needs to do is to move a finger and he will be able to deflect a thousand pounds. This is what it means to keep your body like a well-balanced scale, and to move your waist like a wheel. (TCYQ)

"Strength comes from the bones and is transported through the ligaments. When the ligaments are stretched and elongated, the strength of the bones is increased. When the bones become dense and heavy, the ligaments become agile. When the ligaments are stretched, the bones contract or shrink and become heavy and dense. When the bones become flexible, then their strength has substance and solidity. (TCYQ)

"When your four joints, the two wrists and two ankles,

are stretched through exercises, then your strength will have substance. When you sink your qi and bite your teeth, your bones will become harder. (TCYQ)

B. Stretching

"To stretch the ligaments, we have to stretch the neck, the two wrists and the two ankles. When this is done, then all the ligaments of the body will be elongated.

"To elongate and stretch the neck, bite tightly with the jaws.

"The feet should grasp with the elasticity of a spring.

"The six centers (the two hands, the two feet, the body center and the skull center) must all face each other.

"The chest and back should be rounded. When the back is stretched, it will be strengthened. Then the meridians will be opened and the qi will flow naturally.

"Both upper arms must be stretched horizontally, and both arms must use the following six intentional movements: scooping, embracing, opening, closing, stretching, and contracting.

"The two legs must have the following eight intentional movements: lifting, squeezing (the thighs), scraping (the ground like a dog), pelvis tucked under, knees held in place (over the toes), twisting (both inwardly and outwardly), weight sunk, and spine erect.

"Then your spirit (shen) can rise to the top, and you will

> To stretch the ligaments, we have to stretch the neck, the two wrists and the two ankles. When this is done, then all the ligaments of the body will be elongated.

be in command of your spirit. Your qi, because of the erect posture in which you are standing, will be able to shoot up through the three gates of the spinal chord to the top of the head. In this posture also, your bones will be as strong as the back of a bow, and your ligaments will be stretched like the string of a bow, enabling you to recoil and use your intrinsic strength (jin) fully. (TCYQ)

C. Integration

"All uses of energy are acquired by the individual as a result of experimentation. Therefore, regardless what exercises are used for experimentation or testing, we have first to maintain without broken form. By broken form I mean we must not get out of a sphere with our trunk as the centerline. Intention should not have a form. And strength and energy cannot have direction, because if our strength has direction, then there will be a linear motion which takes us out of our center. This will weaken the strength of the body, and it will become disconnected and confused. Then when it is used in competition with an opponent, it can at best only become like a bullfight, a struggle. Therefore the test of energy must begin in the imagination. Imagination without form can never be broken. It should be like the waves of the ocean. The principle of Quan must come from the void, the emptiness. Yet the spirit must have substance; then the form will be similar to the substance of our spirit. (CEIQ)

Strength and energy cannot have direction, because if our strength has direction, then there will be a linear motion which takes us out of our center.

"Shili (practicing strength) is the most important step toward obtaining boxing skills. Trial of strength (shili) is really the source of force, for one gets to know one's force only by trying one's strength, and only when one has a

93

correct understanding of one's force, can it be applied most effectively. When one first tries strength, its should be balanced, keeping the muscles flexible while letting the bones support firmly the frame of the body. Then the muscles can relax and tense, release and contract freely in close coordination. Strength will be generated internally and discharged externally. (DCQ, p.44)

Fig. 5-4. Wang Xiangzhai

"In the beginning, moving slowly and unhurriedly is better than moving quickly and hurriedly. The slighter the movement, the more fully one's spirit concentrates. You should have the feeling that when you want to stop you continue to move involuntarily and vice versa: that when you want to move you cannot. (DCQ, p.44)

"Lopsided strength is not encouraged; still less, sheer animal strength. The first and foremost thing to do is to perceive intuitively whether the body strength is full and well balanced, whether the strength can be discharged at will and whether one can integrate himself with the air around him to produce reaction. Still more important is that thought should not be interrupted and attention not diverted. (DCQ, p.44)

"Whether one moves forcefully or slightly, one is always able to exert force. Movement of one part of the

94

body is accompanied by movement of every part. As soon as strength reaches it, any given part of the body seems to enter the state of "meditation and wisdom," in which every direction is well taken care of. In a word, unless one obtains comfort, interest, and force, one is not qualified to talk about boxing. (DCQ, p.44)

"The trial of breath is supplementary to the trial of strength. For congenital reasons, physiological structure varies with different people. Each exerciser therefore has particular points in the body that are not easily accessible by strength. This deficiency is made up for by trial of breath, also known as inner breathing, or brain-back breathing exercise. (DCQ, p.44)

4. Fali: Using Strength

"When you release your fist or hand, it will be as if releasing an arrow. When you use your strength, use it as if drawing silk, evenly so as not to break it, while twisting your two hands as if pulling apart cotton. (TCYQ)

> **Your qi can be compared to gunpowder, and your fist to the bullet. Then, using your awareness just a little, it is as if you're pulling the trigger with it, and no flying bird can escape.**

"Your qi can be compared to gunpowder, and your fist to the bullet. Then, using your awareness just a little, it is as if you're pulling the trigger with it, and no flying bird can escape. (TCYQ)

"Self-defense means combat. It should be understood that in actual combat, moving violently is not as good as moving slightly, which again is not as good as not moving at all. It is stillness that is constant movement, just like a flywheel which, when turning extremely fast, looks static. A visible movement is actually nothing but a reflection of weakness. The motion that resides in stillness and looks like stillness is really powerful. Such motion and stillness are interdependent, each being the source of each other. Their magical application depends mainly on the control of the nervous system, the guidance of intention, the contraction and stretching of the joints and ligaments as well as their firm support, the action and reaction of rotating movements, and the use of the elastic force produced in breathing. If all these can be properly used the exerciser can be said to have laid a solid foundation for actual combat. (DCQ, p.44)

Motion and stillness are interdependent, each being the source of each other. Their magical application depends mainly on the control of the nervous system, the guidance of intention, the contraction and stretching of the joints and ligaments...

"What is said here is only something abstract. There are still things that cannot be described with words. But if one goes on practicing boxing with perseverance, they can certainly be perceived in due course. The difference between a violent motion and a slight one varies with the individual and depends on one's foundation, skill, and ability to perceive the mechanism of all forces. If one can perform movements and show mechanical skills every-where, one can move either slightly or violently, or neither slightly nor violently. If one doesn't possess any mechanical skill, movements of whatever kind are of no avail.

"The same is also true of the difference between exerting force and not exerting force. The strength of ordinary people comes from quickened blood circulation only, and such strength is always rigid, divergent, and harmful to health. The strength that doesn't stem from quickened blood circulation is the natural instinctive strength. Such strength will come into play when needed, without effort. Other delicate points such as substantiality and insubstantiality are simply beyond words, and I would not touch this subject here. All in all, Dachengquan is not judged by its mere form, but by the reaction of the mind. All that is visible and tangible is nevertheless illusive. Only when one reaches the realm of freedom and spontaneity will one's skills become really miraculous and formidable. (DCQ, p.45)

5. Radical Criticisms

A. Hsingyiquan

"It must be noted that Xingyiquan in its orthodox form had no such stuff as the "twelve-form exercises," though there should be twelve forms of the body. Nor did it have the theory of mutual promotion and restraint of the five elements. The five elements are only five terms representing five forms of force, not methods or routines of shadow boxing.

"I still remember instructions given by my late masters about the five elements: metal, wood, water, fire and earth. "Metal" refers to the strength in bones and muscle, which is as hard as diamonds and can sever gold or iron. "Wood" refers to the force whose range of action is compared to the supporting shape of a tree. "Water" refers to the force that is like surging ocean and dragon swimming in the sea, penetrating everywhere. "Fire" refers to the force which, like gunpowder, "explodes" and "burns" with a mere touch of the hand. "Earth" refers to the solid, heavy composite force that seems to have been produced by the joint action of the heaven and the earth.

The five elements are only five terms representing five forms of force, not methods or routines of shadow boxing.

"This is what is called "five elements combining into one," not the stuff of one form of boxing overcoming another form of boxing, as some people are preaching nowadays. If one observes first and thinks twice in actual fighting, it is almost certain that he will be defeated long before he takes any action at all. (DCQ, p.39)

B. Taijiquan

"Among disciples by direct line of Taijiquan, I think the most outstanding masterhands are the Yang brothers, Yang Shao Hou and Yang Chengfu. As an intimate friend of theirs, I know that there is indeed some genuine knowledge of mechanics in Taijiquan. However, out of one hundred practitioners, less than one really knows its real essence. Even if one may happen to know some of it, he cannot have a thorough understanding of the whole, because the basic way of perceiving the skill has long been lost, and therefore there is no mechanism of force to speak of in his legwork and footwork.

> I know that there is indeed some genuine knowledge of mechanics in Taijiquan. However, out of one hundred practitioners, less than one really knows its real essence.

"The boxing in question in its original form had only three movements, and was thus called Laosandao (Old Three Cuts). It was changed by Mr. Wang Zongyue and increased to 13 forms, which was further abused to as many as 150 forms. That is one of the main reasons why this boxing has lost its quintessence. If it is practiced for the purpose of preserving one's health, it will only restrain one's spirit and energy and bring discomfort to the practitioner. If practiced for actual combat, it will only do harm to the limbs. Its other functions, if any, are nothing more than idling away the practitioner's time and confusing his mind.

98

Chapter 5 Selected Writings of Wang Xiangzhai

"As to its method of practice, characterized by disoriented blows of the fist and the palm or kicks of foot and leg, I must say it is really ridiculous. In confrontation with a masterhand, such a practitioner of Taijiquan is sure to fail. Even its masterhand, I am afraid, can do nothing with a quite commonplace adversary so long as the latter is not very clumsy. In short, this boxing has been abused to such an extent that it might one day become a mere rigid form like a chess manual.

"In the past twenty years, most practitioners of Taijiquan have not been aware of its falseness. Even if someone is clearheaded, he does not know what he should actually do. As to ordinary learners, most of them believe in what is heard without using their own eyes. Thus Taijiquan is in fact being pushed towards its graveyard. What a great loss! I sincerely hope those competent followers of that boxing will straighten it out and make it systematic, with a view to developing it in the future. Here I have taken the liberty of making comments on Taijiquan, and I don't know whether my comments are appropriate. Pardon me if I am too outspoken. I think one day those learners of Taijiquan who have really gained something would agree with me in this regard. (DCQ, p.40)

Taijiquan is in fact being pushed towards its graveyard. What a great loss! I sincerely hope those competent followers of that boxing will straighten it out and make it systematic, with a view to developing it in the future.

C. Baguazhang

"Bagua (eight trigrams) was formerly known as quanzhang (Palm of Siquan Province). I once had an interview with Mr. Cheng Tinghua. When he was performing the feat, he was, as I recall, like a divine dragon roaming, winding and twisting in the sky. Such superb skills are really beyond the reach of us contemporaries. As to Master Dong Haichuan's boxing, it is even more difficult to have a true understanding of his skills. Mr. Liu Fengchun is a friend of mine. He has acquired remarkable skills, though his attainment is not so great as Master Dong. Even so, he is far superior to the practitioners of "64 palms" or "72 kicks." I hope that those who practice Bagua will concentrate on single and double palm forms, and try their best to perceive every movement. At the same time, they should make a penetrating study of the theory and put it into practice." (DCQ, p.40)

Part III

The Tao (Yang) of Yiquan

Chapter 6

Zhanzhuang and the Structure of Stillness

1. Master Han Comes to America

At a grand dinner party in 1997 celebrating his group's twentieth year of standing practice, Master Fong Ha recounted his involvement in bringing Yiquan from China to the U.S. "In my early days of researching and studying the Chinese martial arts, I met Mr. Sam Tam of Vancouver, Canada. Sam later became my lifelong friend and fellow student of the art, and introduced me to the study of Yiquan. With his letter of introduction I went to Hong Kong in the early seventies and met my teacher-to-be, Master Han Xingyuen, one of the major disciples of Master Wang Xiangzhai, the founder of Yiquan.... Finally, during the summers of 1976 and 1977 I invited Master Han to stay with my family in San Francisco. I wanted to share with all my friends and students Master Han's deep knowledge."[1]

Fig. 6-1.
Master Fong Ha

Fig. 6-2.
Master Sam Tam

This turned out to be a pivotal event in my own personal development. With the coming of Master Han, my education regarding the relationship of martial arts and meditation was about to be accelerated beyond the comfortable into the painful.

One thing I had really liked about Master Fong Ha's personality from the very beginning was his easy tolerance and acceptance of people's basic natures. This feature appealed to many counterculture types, who were into "self-development" and "doing one's

Fig. 6-3. Master
Han Xingyuen

own thing." So even though he himself practiced his art relentlessly, he never attempted to force, or even promote, his own practice habits with his students. This left them entirely free to define their own level of commitment, resulting in quite a mixed bag of people, where commitment ran the gamut from the deep to the perfunctory.

Master Han, however, was of the old school—brooking no nonsense. His basic attitude was: If you're coming to study with me, you do what I tell you and for as long as I tell you to do it; otherwise, you're not going to do it with me at all." So I did what he told me to do and for as long as he told me to do it, and I suffered. Of the two things I learned from him—stillness and movement—the suffering that took place in the stillness training irrevocably changed my life.

2. Practice with Master Han

The minimum standing session with Master Han was 40 minutes: five minutes for each of eight postures. This was followed by 20 to 30 minutes of stationary movement practice and an equal amount of time practicing walking movement patterns.

I emphasize here the word "minimum" for often visitors would come and engage Sifu (the Chinese term for teacher) in such a way that he kind of forgot about us and simply left us standing there—holding the ball so to speak. This way the zhanzhuang (pile) standing sessions often stretched beyond an hour, even approaching an hour and a half.

The standing practice was always done with the group

> Master Han was of the old school—brooking no nonsense. His basic attitude was: If you're coming to study with me you do what I tell you and for as long as I tell you to do it; otherwise you're not going to do it with me at all.

standing in a circle. Sifu would walk by and individually adjust each person with each posture. Frequently, he would make you sit lower than you thought possible, and always subtly turn the arms in such a way that they wanted to fall off and separate from your body almost immediately.

Fig. 6-4.   Master Han and some of the early-morning group

The time of practice was always early: 7am. When Master Han first came, the location of practice was Fong's house in the Sunset district in San Francisco. When he came the second time, a year later, the location shifted to Golden Gate Park. The time of day and the cold weather added immeasurably to the difficulty of the ordeal.

Standing for close to an hour with my knees deeply bent and my arms stretched out in front of me in the freezing cold while not moving a muscle, I questioned my sanity more than once. My legs were shaking, my arms so

Fig. 6-5. Master Han in postures #1 - #4

Fig. 6-6. Master Han in postures #5 - #8

tired they felt like they were going to drop off any moment. I didn't even bother to lower them because I knew Sifu would just come over and raise them back up in front of my chest, and probably force my torso to sit even lower on my shaking legs. All the while he would look at me with impenetrable eyes and a half-smile, speaking silent volumes in a language I didn't understand.

Fig. 6-7. Master Han and the author

I understood enough, however, to realize that I was being subjected to a "sink or swim" method of training. So besides a kind of innate stubbornness and refusal to give up, the thing that kept me going was a true desire to "break on through to the other side" where a transformed body and mind would open up new realms of skill and ecstatic experience.

3. Therapeutic Discoveries

Almost from the moment I began the practice of standing meditation, my body reacted rebelliously and violently. At first, the musculature of my body simply was not developed and strong enough to meet the demands of holding the positions, resulting in an intense trembling of the musculature and involuntary, often violent, shaking of the body.

Yet, even as I developed the physical strength to maintain the postures, this shaking continued. Physically and psychologically I got literally "all shook up." Recollec-

Chapter 6   Zhanzhuang and the Structure of Stillness

tions of childhood trauma and associated fears and angers began to surface during bouts of shaking. These I interpreted, in accordance with my Reichian and bioenergetic perspective, as the therapeutic process of dissolving specific myofascial blockages in the body armor. Thus, working through the agony of the standing and shaking became an integral part of a therapeutic journey. It became my path of resolving old traumas and contradictions while opening the energy pathways and reintegrating the body's segments, or springs.

In a nutshell, my developmental experience in the Yiquan system attests to the truth of the old adage that the agony precedes the ecstasy. In my case the requisite process of breaking up psychosomatic blockages through the shaking was agonizing indeed. The subsequent experience of reintegrating the segmented parts of the body with each other and with the mind has, over the years, been an endless source of ecstasy.

Working through the agony of the standing and shaking became an integral part of a therapeutic journey. It became my path of resolving old traumas and contradictions while opening the energy pathways and reintegrating the body.

My developmental process in the art of standing was marked by a series of experiential discoveries I will describe in the pages that follow. First, I discovered the truth that integral strength is acquired through the proper integration of the body's three springs. Second, I discovered that learning to relax and root properly gives this strength its peculiar elastic and explosive qualities. Third, I realized that the yin-yang of tension/relaxation is the primary pulse of life itself. Fourth, I realized that the Yiquan practice, ultimately a method of mastering the pulse of life, is based on understanding the inter-penetration of yin and yang in which strength is produced from within relaxation, and relaxation occurs within the use of strength.

4. Pile Standing

From a strictly mechanical and anatomical point of view the zhanzhuang standing meditation practice of Yiquan is first and foremost a method of readying the body's three springs—foundation (legs), torso (centerline) and sphere (arms)—for unified action directed by the mind (yi). We begin with a description and analysis of the functioning of the torso spring.

Yiquan is first and foremost a method of readying the body's three springs— foundation (legs), torso (centerline) and sphere (arms)—for unified action directed by the mind.

The first essential awareness Yiquan practice cultivates is of the rooting and verticality of our body cylinder. Indeed, zhanzhuang is most appropriately translated as "pile standing" to encourage our experience of our body being as solidly rooted as a piling that is driven into the ground.

The cylindrical nature of the body is a feature the human species shares with most animal species. The upright position of this cylinder is, however, quite unique to the human species. Its evolutionary advantages have often been pointed out: Upright posture freed the fore-limbs for grasping and manipulating, which in turn profoundly favored the evolution of brain and mind.

But there is also a downside to the enormous evolutionary advantages the adoption of upright bipedal posture and gait gave the human species. Compared with our animal cousins, our equilibrium and balance became a much more complicated and precarious affair. There is no getting away from the fact that a vertical cylinder balanced on two supporting limbs is inherently a great deal less stable than a horizontal cylinder balanced on four supporting limbs.

110

Chapter 6   Zhanzhuang and the Structure of Stillness

The practice of Yiquan zhanzhuang addresses this challenge directly by cultivating systematic enhancement and control over our kinesthetic sense of equilibrium. The practice of pile standing must be a prerequisite to the practice of movement. The extent to which we have learned to optimize the relationship of our body cylinder to gravity in a stationary position will determine the quality of our movement.

5. Centerline

Primary among the factors that determine the optimal stability of the human cylinder is the proper perpendicular alignment of the cylinder's centerline to gravity and the earth's surface. Any cylinder, human or otherwise, has a longitudinal centerline. The more closely the actual position of the centerline approaches the ideal perpendicular position, the more stable the cylinder will be. Simply put, the tower of Pisa, for example, is not to be taken as a model of structural stability. Likewise in zhanzhuang practice, we continually try to approach optimal stability of our cylinder by cultivating ever-greater awareness of ever-smaller deviations from the ideal and correcting our posture and stances accordingly.

In zhanzhuang practice, we continually try to approach optimal stability of our cylinder by cultivating ever-greater awareness of ever-smaller deviations from the ideal and correcting our posture and stances accordingly.

The proper internal structure of the human cylinder and centerline is also paramount in maintaining optimal balance and equilibrium. The human cylinder is flexible and has an internal structure provided by the spine and its associated musculature. The spine has four curves: sacral, lumbar, thoracic, and cervical. Of these four, the sacral and thoracic curves are the more rigid, and the lumbar and cervical are the more flexible.

111

In ideal posture, the four curves are related to each other in such a way as to equalize and maximize the load distribution of the torso in relationship to gravity around its centerline. In the actual posture of most human beings there is serious impairment of the structural integrity and alignment of the spine, imposing extra stresses and tensions on the associated musculature, and resulting in malformations of the human cylinder and a corresponding decrease of stable vertical equilibrium. See *Figs. 6-8 and 6-9.*

6. Centerpoint

In a remarkable and most meaningful coincidence, our center of gravity is also the center, or origin, of biological growth.

The human body not only has a centerline, but also a centerpoint, which is the very center of our gravity. It is located midway up the centerline, measured from the top of the head to the ground, in the horizontal middle of the cylinder. It is slightly below the navel and just above the sacrum.

In a remarkable and most meaningful coincidence, our center of gravity is also the center, or origin, of biological growth. The human fetus, like all other animals, unfolds equally up and down from the center at the top of the sacrum. Undoubtedly, the ancients intuited this very truth when they gave the name "Os sacrum" to this bone, since it literally means "holy bone."

A further point of great significance is that the human centerpoint is the point of relative integration or disintegration between the upper and lower halves of the torso or cylinder. It is the point of the greatest structural defects in the spine and source of the greatest number of postural aberrations. For that reason, much time is spent in Yiquan zhanzhuang meditation cultivating internal awareness of the centerpoint as the very point for reintegration of the upper and lower torso.

7. Activating the Torso Spring

In the work of Yiquan, it is possible and necessary to realign the spine and reprogram the associated musculature to achieve optimum structural integrity, verticality, flexibility and strength. In order to do so, the torso spring is activated, and the upper and lower parts of the spine are reintegrated by aligning top and bottom tips of the spine with the centerline.

In the work of Yiquan, it is possible and necessary to realign the spine and reprogram the associated musculature to achieve optimum structural integrity, verticality, flexibility, and strength.

Alignment entails going from convexity to concavity by using the pelvic tilt to pull the coccyx forward and up, tucking the chin, pulling back the ears, and pushing up the top of the head. This has the effect of restoring the central spinal joint by pushing out the mingmen (the point between the second and third lumbar vertebrae) and eliminating the lumbar spinal curve.

We must look at both the top and bottom ends of the spine and align them properly. This means paying attention to the two most flexible spinal curves, the cervical and the lumbar, which are also the two most likely to be frozen in habitually deficient and inefficient postural misalignment.

Wang Xiangzhai reminds us time and again to avoid arching the back and to keep it straight. We must "tuck the pelvis under" so that we will be able to find "the source of our strength in expanding our lower back." By the same token, he admonishes us to "keep the head straight [and] avoid the habit of tilting the head back, because that also breaks the straightness of the back."

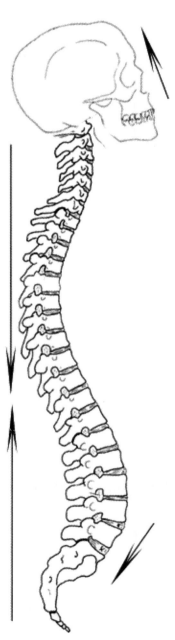

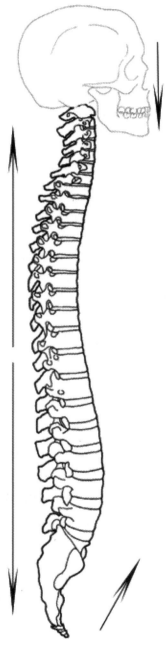

Fig. 6-8. Normal, pathological spine with excessive curvatures

Fig. 6-9 Natural, healthy spine with minimal curvatures cultivated in zhanzhuang

8. Foundation

Our center is related to our root through gravity. In outer space, in the absence of the earth's gravity, the human cylinder in fact proves itself to be a human sphere, as all our movement revolves around and emanates from our center of gravity in the lower trunk. If we want to control our movement in outer space, we must control our center of gravity. On Earth, our foundation or base grounds our center to Earth's center of gravity. Therefore, movement on Earth starts in our rootedness.

The stability of the human centerline is only as good as the foundation that supports it. The proper relationship of the cylinder of the human torso to its foundation—legs and feet—is therefore of utmost importance. In zhanzhuang meditation, scrupulous attention is paid to maintaining the proper position of legs and feet to provide the optimally stable structure to root the centerline.

The stability of the human centerline is only as good as the foundation that supports it.

The feet are placed parallel, shoulderwidth apart, resembling the figure eleven or representing two parallel sides of a square box. This is the middle way, neither pointing outward as in splayed feet, nor pointing inward as in pigeon-toedness. And the feet should "grasp the ground with the elasticity of a spring," and be ready to "scrape the ground like a dog…[with)]the tips of the toes slightly extended."

The knees also keep to the middle way, neither totally bent nor totally straight and kept in place thrusting forward over the toes while sinking the heel into the ground. Also, in imagination, one has a balloon between the knees that is expanding outward, putting the weight on the outside of the feet. Keeping the outwardly expanding sensation of the knees, one equalizes the weight between the inside and outside of both feet. The isometric tension thus created in the legs stabilizes the foundation (leg and foot) structure and therefore provides a secure base from which the torso and centerline can operate.

9. Sphere

In the universal post or pile stance the arms are held as if they are embracing a tree or holding a large round object, such as a beach ball, in front of the chest.

Regarding the position of arms and hands in the universal post posture while doing zhanzhuang practice, Wang Xiangzhai's writings only instruct us to place the hands "somewhere in front of the body between belly and chest level." The lack of preciseness in his directions underlines the fact that Wang Xiangzhai considered the awareness of essence as ultimately more important than the technical details.

In the universal post or pile stance the arms are held as if they are embracing a tree or holding a large round object, such as a beach ball, in front of the chest. Following the maxim of "rounding the shoulders and hollowing the chest," the shoulders are relaxed (down) and rounded, intent first extending them out laterally to the side and then curving them slightly forwards. Or, as Wang Xiangzhai himself expressed it, the upper arms "should be stretched horizontally, using the following six intentional movements: scooping, embracing, opening, closing, stretching, and contracting." The elbows "neither straight nor overly bent," with the tips of the fingers extending slightly, as if each hand is holding a rather large ball.[2]

Chapter 6   Zhanzhuang and the Structure of Stillness

10. Nervous System Integration

The most primitive portion of the mammalian nervous system, the spinal cord, mediates the most basic postural reflexes. In all mammals, including man, merely putting pressure on the bottoms of the feet activates spinal postural reflexes that stiffen and strengthen the legs and spine to provide the minimum structure necessary for standing.[3]

At the next higher level of nervous integration, the pons and the brain stem coordinate information from the semi-circular canals in the inner ear (the sensory organ for gravitational perceptions and balance) with the spinal cord's postural reflexes.[4] Through this mechanism, a rigid, fixed posture is made more flexible and at the same time more stable, because compensating adjustments among the simple postural reflexes is now possible."[5]

Standing meditation is the work of bringing deep unconscious reflexes and processes into consciousness. By paying attention to and correlating proprioceptive and kinesthetic data, we seek to hone these instinctual abilities to a fine edge.

In all mammals these mechanism operate instinctually and automatically. Even in man they generally operate below the level of neo-cortical awareness, even though due to our bipedal gait, relatively speaking, an inordinately large portion of our brain is concerned with maintaining balance and equilibrium.

In the final analysis, standing meditation is the work of bringing these deep unconscious reflexes and processes into consciousness. Indeed, by paying attention to and correlating proprioceptive and kinesthetic data, we seek to hone these instinctual abilities to a fine edge.

Chapter 7

Polarity and the Grammar of Movement

1. Introduction

Owing to our upright, bipedal stance, the centerline of the human torso cylinder is vertical and rooted to the ground by means of the legs, as foundation. Yiquan begins the derivation of its grammar, or rules, of human movement through meditation on the action of the foundation spring. This because the function of the foundation spring is to initiate and propel the movement of the human centerline (CL) and torso through space.

As defined by the polarities and orientation of our bodies in three-dimensional space, the experiential content of standing practice reveals three possible elementary movements of the centerline:

    1. **Vertical movement.** The up-down polarity of our structure gives rise to the ability to lower and raise the CL.

    2. **Horizontal movement.** The front-back polarity allows shifting the CL from foot to foot in walking.

    3. **Rotational movement.** The left-right polarity allows for the rotation of the CL clockwise and counter-clockwise.

In the universal, or pile stance, meditation posture, the centerline is positioned so as to be in the middle of the spectrum defined by each of these three polarities. By unlocking and bending the knees somewhat, the centerline is neither lowered nor raised to its maximum capacity, but

The experiential content of standing practice reveals three possible elementary movements of the centerline: vertical movement, horizontal movement, and rotational movement.

119

kept in the middle. The weight of the body is distributed equally between both legs, again favoring the middle of balance between the two extremes. Lastly, the centerline is neither rotated clockwise nor counterclockwise, but is maintained in the middle.

The three main joints of the foundation of the legs—ankles, knees, and hips—interact intimately in all three types of movement. Nevertheless, each joint is primary in one of the centerline's movements, while being supportive in the other two. The knees are primary in allowing the lowering and raising of the centerline. The ankle is primary in the shifting and smooth transference of weight and centerline from one foot to the other. The hips are primary in rotational movement around the centerline. In Yiquan practice, awareness of the fundamental mechanisms involved in these functional relationships is refined to an unusually high degree, leading to exquisite control over our bodily movements.

If I let my body move naturally with the breath, the torso would sink a little as I exhaled and rise a little as I inhaled.

2. Vertical CL movement

I first became aware of the vertical dimension of CL movement as a result of simply watching my breath. This can easily be verified by anyone. I noticed that if I let my body move naturally with the breath, the torso would sink a little as I exhaled and rise a little as I inhaled. In this behavior the human body acts very much like the balloon that it is. It will sink as air is allowed to escape, and will rise when more air is taken in.

Michael Mayer, fellow traveler on the path of standing meditation, described his discovery of the sinking-rising

120

action of the breath during a scuba diving experience. He noticed that 50 feet or so down he was "standing in the water…in equilibrium between sinking and rising to the surface…arms floating free with no tension, every joint in the body loosened as I became one with the water…. As the breath came into my lungs, they inflated like a balloon, and I started to rise in the water…. As I breathed out and my lungs deflated, I sank down five, ten, fifteen feet."[1]

Thus the first Yiquan movement exercise derives from the breathing cycle and involves the vertical movement of the CL. To adhere to the spirit of Yiquan as the System of the Mind, I will refer to each body action described as an "awareness exercise" rather than an "exercise."

Awareness exercise 7-1. Stand in parallel stance with arms hanging by the sides, also known as the wuji posture. Allow the torso to sink and relax into the foundation of the legs as you exhale and let the air out, and allow the torso

> **As the breath came into my lungs, they inflated like a balloon, and I started to rise in the water…. As I breathed out and my lungs deflated, I sank down five, ten, fifteen feet.**

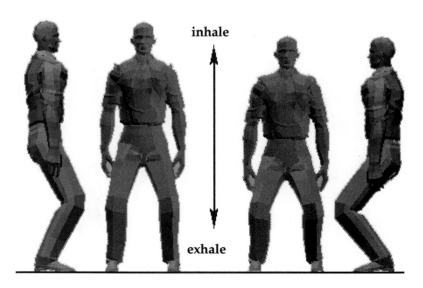

inhale

exhale

Ex. 7-1. Vertical centerline movement with breath

to rise as you inhale and take the air in. Pay careful attention to maintaining the verticality of the CL: do not wobble or bend it, nor let it lean forward, backward, or sideways. In order to make conscious and reinforce in us the fundamental connection between breath and movement, this exercise is repeated over and over. The relaxed sinking on the exhalation is the method of developing deep rootedness and stability of the foundation by relaxing hips, knees, and ankles.

Yiquan seeks to understand the world of phenomena in terms of polarity. Accordingly, if something is done one way, it is instructive to attempt to do it the opposite way.

Awareness exercise 7-2. Reverse the breathing cycle and the vertical movement of the CL. Inhale as you sink the CL, loading the spring of the legs, and exhale as you raise the CL, releasing the spring of the legs. Imagine taking the energy of the breath down into the feet as you inhale and sink, and imagine pushing the energy back up

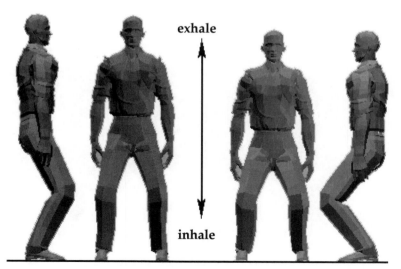

exhale

inhale

Ex. 7-2. Vertical centerline movement with reverse breath

and out the body when you exhale and raise the body up.

3. Horizontal CL movement

Equilibrium of the centerline is not a static condition we can take for granted, but a dynamic event even in stillness, maintained largely by unconscious processes. Standing practice brings these processes to consciousness. The heightened sense of balance acquired is then re-applied and expanded into conscious movement practice.

Simply trying to keep the weight evenly distributed fifty-fifty between both legs in standing meditation is an extremely difficult task. When you try it, you will notice that there is a constantly changing microdifferential—that you are minutely shifting back and forth from foot to foot, as well as from balls to heels of the feet.

Simply trying to keep the weight evenly distributed between both legs in standing meditation is an extremely difficult task.

The second CL movement is derived from the fundamental polarity of left-right symmetry and bipedality. It consists of shifting the CL from foot to foot in a horizontal plane of movement. In parallel stance, this involves left-right, side-to-side horizontal movement. We will see later that in the structurally more complicated archer step, the forward/backward polarity is also involved.

Awareness exercise 7-3. Now do this shifting exercise in parallel stance. Make the stance a little wider than shoulder width; this makes it easier to pay close attention to the shifting of CL. Be careful to keep the CL plumb and do not lean it as you shift back and forth. Notice that as you shift, the weight wants to go to the outside of the foot

Ex. 7-3. Horizontal centerline movement

you're shifting onto and to the inside of the foot you're shifting from. Correct these tendencies as they occur, always keeping the weight even between the inside and outside of each foot. Notice how this stabilizes the foundation of the legs while shifting the CL.

Also harmonize the breathing with the CL shifting movement.

Also harmonize the breathing with the CL shifting movement. It is not so much that there is a particular right way to breathe as that you are paying attention and making a connection between breath and movement. Often I follow the pattern of inhaling as I shift to center and exhaling when I shift to one foot. I also frequently use the pattern of holding my center still over one foot as I inhale, and using the exhale to traverse and shift the CL the whole distance to the other foot.

4. Rotational CL movement

The third CL movement is also derived from the unique characteristic of human posture. Being a vertical cylinder balanced on a bipedal base allows the torso to rotate around its axis in either clockwise or counterclockwise direction. Simply put, unlike our mammalian cousins who move on all fours, we humans are able to rotate the body to the left and to the right.

Awareness exercise 7-4. In parallel stance, fix the knees over the feet by imagining holding a ball between them. Then slowly rotate left and right. Keep shoulders and hips aligned so as not to twist the spine. Harmonize the breath as in shifting: inhale when rotating to neutral, square position, exhale on the rotation to either side. Or, alternatively, hold the rotated position as you inhale, and then exhale during the entire rotation to the other side.

The third CL movement is the ability of the torso to rotate around its axis in either clockwise or counterclockwise direction.

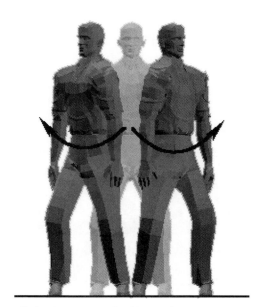

Ex. 7-4. Rotational Centerline Movement

5. Functional stances

Those stances that have the feet in parallel position are considered cultivational or health stances. Those stances in which one foot is placed in front of the other are for use in fighting, and are therefore called functional stances.

Many Yiquan practitioners make a functional stance their main method of zhazhong practice. For example the great Yiquan artist, Kuo Lin Ying, who taught for decades in San Francisco, exclusively used and taught a 100%-rear-weighted universal stance.

The length of the stance and the distribution of the weight can be varied according to purpose. For power training and rooting, the stances may be low and long with weight on both feet for the most part; for readiness and agility, stances are usually high, with 90-100% of the weight on the rear foot.

Ex. 7-5. Various functional stances

Awareness exercise 7-5. Vertical CL movement practice in functional stance. Begin with a moderately small stance, placing one foot a foot-length in front of the other. First practice the up-down movements of the CL with weight 50% on rear foot and 50% on front (50/50). Then practice them with 70% on rear foot and 30 % on front. Also with 30% on rear foot and 70% on front. Then also practice them with 90-100% on the rear foot. Finally, do the same with a larger stance, placing front foot two foot-lengths in front of rear foot.

Awareness exercise 7-6. Practice horizontal movement of the CL, shifting CL back and forth in short and longer functional stances.

Awareness exercise 7-7. Practice rotational movements of the CL with weight 50/50, 70% on rear foot and 30% on front, 30% on rear foot and 70% on front, and 90-100% on the rear and front foot each.

Awareness exercise 7-8. Improvise and combine. Now take any parallel or functional stance and begin combining the vertical, horizontal and rotational CL movements into different patterns.

6. Walking

Walking is shifting with the addition of stepping. Stepping is placing the foot by extending the leg.

Awareness exercise 7-9. Practice placing the foot forward, sideways, backward, and diagonally in many different positions without wobbling and compromising CL stability.

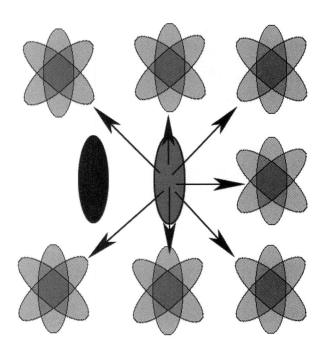

Ex. 7-9. Stepping exercise

Awareness exercise 7-10. In walking forward, first the foot is extended forward and placed on the ground before the CL and weight is committed to shift onto it. The moment the forward foot is placed on the ground it lightly pushes back into the rear foot. This stabilizes the movement by creating a small isometric tension between front and rear leg. Then maintaining that pressure evenly, commit the weight and shift the center to the front foot by pushing from the rear. Repeat procedure to step and shift with the other foot.

(The forward foot pushing back lightly)...stabilizes the movement by creating a small isometric tension between front and rear leg.

In placing the foot forward, it is always first brought in next to the rooted one before being extended. This results in walking by dragging the feet in a half-circle. This type of walking is also called a rubbing or grinding step, depending on the amount of friction used, because the sole of the foot stays in touch with the ground.

Awareness exercise 7-11. Harmonize the stepping and shifting with the breathing cycle. Inhale as you step and exhale as you shift.

Walking exercise, like standing and stationary movement, can be practiced three ways: high, medium and low. The primary method of walking is in a high stance with small steps, feet parallel. This gives the greatest agility. Medium-stance walking uses a slightly longer step, with the rear foot turned out a bit. It gives up some agility in favor of greater stability. Low-stance walking uses an even longer, lower stance in which the rear foot is naturally turned out even more. It sacrifices agility for the greatest stability.

The primary method of walking is in a high stance with small steps, feet parallel. This gives the greatest agility.

Awareness exercise 7-12. Walking backward. The same procedure is used in walking backward as in walking forward. Reach, feel, and place the foot backward in a semi-circle, then commit the weight by shifting the CL.

Ex. 7-10. - 12. Walking exercise

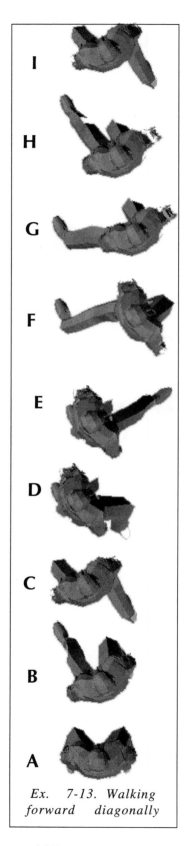

Ex. 7-13. Walking forward diagonally

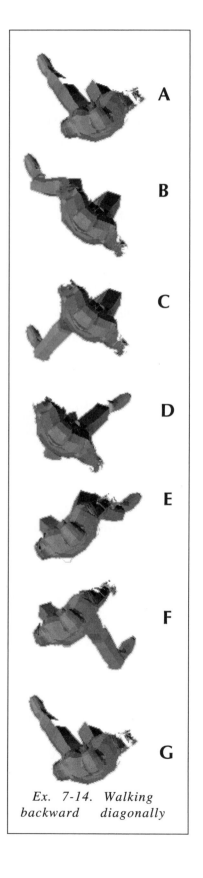

Ex. 7-14. Walking backward diagonally

Chapter 7 Polarity and the Grammar of Movement

7. Turning

Awareness exercise 7-13. Changing directions. Changing directions involves both rotation of the torso CL and rotation of the leg cylinder. Practice 90-degree change of direction by means of diagonal walking. Begin from a parallel stance (A), and fix the CL over the right foot. Rotate 45 degrees to the left and place the left foot pointing diagonally to the corner (B). Then shift the CL and fix it over the left foot (C) and rotate torso 90 degrees to face the right corner (D). Pull the right foot in and place it pointing into the right corner(E); adjust left foot if necessary. Then shift the CL and fix it over the right foot(F) and rotate torso 90 degrees to face the left corner(G). Pull the left foot in and place it pointing into the left corner(H); adjust right foot if necessary. Shift the CL over the left foot (I)... Repeat 10,000 times.

Awareness exercise 7-14. Do the same walking backward diagonally. For example, with the CL on the right foot (A), rotate torso to right front corner (B). Pull in left foot and place it to the left rear, i.e. opposite corner (C). Then commit the weight and shift CL onto rear left foot (D). Adjust front right foot as needed. Then rotate torso to left front corner (E). Pull in right foot and place it in right rear, i.e. opposite corner (F). Then commit the weight and shift CL onto rear right foot (G/A). Adjust front left foot as needed. Then rotate torso to right front corner (B). Pull in left foot and place it to the left rear, i.e. opposite corner (C). ...Repeat 10,000 times.

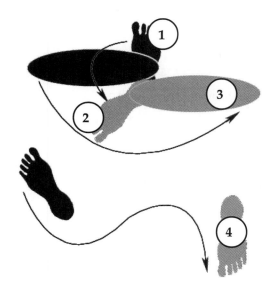

Ex. 7-15. Turning 180 degrees

Awareness exercise 7-15. This is the default method of turning 180 degrees or more from a functional stance. Assume right foot in front (1). Fix the CL over the heel of the right foot and simultaneously rotate the right leg by toeing in 135 degrees (2) and rotating the torso to the left 180 degrees (counterclockwise) (3). Pick up left foot and place pointing 180 degrees in opposite direction (4). Adjust right foot if necessary. Then repeat for other side. Fix the CL over the heel of the left foot and simultaneously rotate the left leg by toeing in 135 degrees and rotating the torso to the right 180 degrees (clockwise). Pick up right foot and place, pointing 180 degrees in the opposite direction. Adjust left foot if necessary. Repeat over and over.

8. Movement of the Sphere

Taking our cue from Wang Xiangzhai, the essential structure of the sphere of the arms in the universal stance is determined by the extremes of four fundamental polarity structures. Just as we discovered there were three fundamental polarity structures that define the movement of the CL and torso, the arms in the universal stance represent the middle way, or resting point, between the four polarity structures that define the experience and movement of the human sphere. The polarities are as follows:

A. **extension-retraction**

B. **inversion-eversion**

C. **up-down**

D. **opening-closing.**

The polarities of the sphere have their origin in the structure of three-dimensional space and biological function.

The polarities of the sphere have their origin in the structure of three-dimensional space and biological function. The primary function of our arms and hands is to control our environment by literally manipulating it. The purpose of arm spring flexion is to take things from the environment and bring them close to us, as in eating or embracing a loved one. The extension of the arm spring is to keep the environment from embracing or invading us by the repelling action of pushing it away. Thus the first polarity of the sphere is towards-away from the body. The universal pose represents the middle way, neither fully extended, nor fully flexed.

To emphasize the fact that we are trying here to become acquainted with the structure and function of the sphere in itself, the following awareness exercises are done sitting on a stool. This is also expressive of the fact

THE TAO OF YIQUAN

that sitting meditation is an essential part of the practice of Yiquan. In the next chapter we will integrate the possibilities of movement of the sphere with the possibilities of movement of foundation and CL to arrive at an integrated description of movement of the body as a whole.

Sitting meditation is an essential part of the practice of Yiquan.

A. Extension-retraction

Awareness exercise 7-16. The first polarity of the sphere is extension-retraction. From the universal pose (B), alternately extend the arms away from (A) and retract them towards the body (C). At first keep your body stable and unmoving, so that all movement occurs only in the arms. When holding the universal pose still, cultivate awareness of the possibilities of this movement.

Awareness exercise 7-17. Keep the elbows fixed in space and use them as the fulcrum of movement. Experi-

The first polarity of the sphere is exten-sion-retraction.

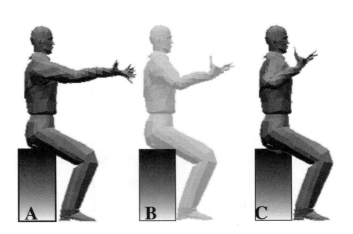

Ex. 7-16. Universal Pose(B), Extended (A), Retracted (C)

ence the equal expansion forward by the hands and forearms and backward with the upper arms and torso. When holding the universal pose still, cultivate awareness of the possibilities of this movement.

134

Ex. 7-17. Using the elbows as fulcrum in extending-contracting the sphere

B. Inversion-eversion

The second polarity of the sphere (inversion-eversion) is derived from the rotational ability of the forearms. This specifically human biological specialization aids manipulation, allowing inversion-eversion of the palms towards and away from the body, as we do in grasping and bringing something to our mouth, or pushing away an unwanted advance. Here too, the universal pose represents the middle way. The forearms are held at the midpoint between greatest possible inversion (turning in) and eversion (turning out).

The second polarity of the sphere (inversion-eversion) is derived from the rotational ability of the forearms.

Awareness exercise 7-18. In the universal pose, slowly rotate forearms from one extreme to another.

front   side

Ex. 7-18. Inverting and everting the sphere

135

When holding the universal pose still, cultivate awareness of the possibilities of this movement. In terms of Master Han's postures in the previous chapter, this is going from #1 to #2.

Awareness exercise 7-19. Combine exercises #17 (and #18) with #19. Retract your arms while turning forearms and palms towards you; extend your arms while turning forearms and palms away from you.

Ex. 7-19. Inverting while retracting and everting while extending the sphere

The third polarity of the sphere is the up-down of vertical movement.

C. Up-down

The third polarity of the sphere is the up-down of vertical movement. Here too the arms are held at the midpoint (Ex.7-20A) between greatest possible lowering (Ex.7-20B) and greatest possible raising (Ex.7-20C).

Awareness exercise 7-20. From the universal pose, slowly lower arms to their minimum (Ex.7-20B) next to the legs and slowly raise them to the maximum above the head (Ex.7-20C). When holding the universal pose still, cultivate awareness of the possibilities of this movement.

Ex.   7-20.   Raising and lowering of the sphere

Awareness exercise 7-21. In the universal pose, fix the elbows, and using them as fulcrum, lower and raise only the forearms. When holding the universal pose still, cultivate awareness of the possibilities of this movement. This is moving from Master Han's # 1 to # 3 posture.

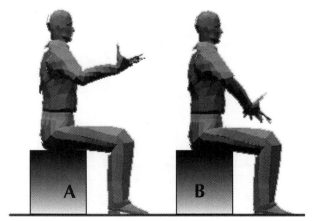

Ex. 7-21. Raising and lowering of
the sphere from #1 (A) to #3 posture (B)

Awareness exercise 7-22. Move from Master Han's #1 to #3 posture by rotating the forearms.

Ex. 7-22. Rotating the sphere from #3 (A) to # 4 posture (B)

Awareness exercise 7-23. Combine exercises19 with 21 and 22. Turn the palms up when raising the (fore)arms as if lifting something, and turn the palms down when lowering the (fore)arms as if pushing down on something.

Ex. 7-23. Raising and lowering of the sphere from #1 (A) to #4 posture (B)

D. Opening-closing.

The fourth polarity of the sphere derives from human bilateral symmetry. Here again, the arms are held at the midpoint *(Ex.7-24A)* between the greatest opening out laterally *(Ex.7-24B)* from the centerline and the greatest closing in towards the centerline *(Ex.7-24C)*.

Awareness exercise 7-24. From the universal pose, slowly open the arms to the sides as far as you can, and then close them until you are hugging yourself. When holding the universal pose still, cultivate awareness of the possibilities of this movement.

Ex. 7-24.   Opening and closing the sphere.

Awareness exercise 7-25. While holding #1 posture utilize the polarities of opening-closing and extending-retracting to move the hands with small horizontal circles in front of their respective shoulders. Open while retracting *(Ex.7-25B)* and close while extending *(Ex.7-25A)*.

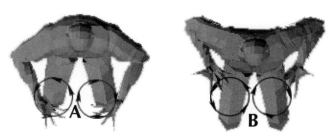

Ex.   7-25. Making horizontal circles

Awareness exercise 7-26. Now add the rotation polarity. As you retract and open, turn the forearms to #1 position *(Ex.7-26B)*. As you extend and close, turn the forearms to #2 position *(Ex.7-26A)*.

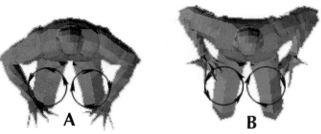

Ex. 7-26. Making horizontal cicles with forearm rotation

In all the movements generated by the four polarities of the sphere described so far, the two arms have acted synchronously, doing the same thing. Now experience the movement generated by these polarities when the hands are working oppositionally, each doing the opposite thing.

Awareness exercise 7-27. From the universal pose, alternately extend and retract the arms. As you retract the right, extend the left and vice versa.

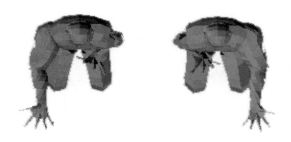

Ex. 7-27 Alternately extending and retracting

Chapter 7 Polarity and the Grammar of Movement

Awareness exercise 7-28. From the universal pose, alternately lower and raise the arms. As you raise the right, lower the left and vice versa.

Ex. 7-28 Alternately raising and lowering

Awareness exercise 7-29. From the universal pose, alternately evert and invert the palms. As you evert the right, invert the left and vice versa.

Ex. 7-29. Alternately inverting and everting forearms

Awareness exercise 7-30. From the universal pose, alternately open and close the arms. As you open the right, close the left and vice versa.

Ex. 7-30. Alternately opening and closing

It is beyond the scope of this work to list all the possible combinations and permutations, so this investigative task will be left to the reader/practitioner. A good place to begin, however, is by combining alternate forearm rotation with the movements of alternate extension-retraction, up-down and opening-closing of the sphere.

In summary, the genius of the Yiquan system is that it presents a grammar of movement, a metasystem applicable to all other systems as well as to itself.

First, the three elemental, or primary, movements of the centerline combine in endless permutations to create an infinity of vertical, horizontal and rotational circles of the torso and CL.

Chapter 7 Polarity and the Grammar of Movement

Second, the four polarities of the sphere combine in endless permutations to create an infinity of vertical, horizontal and rotational circles of the sphere.

Third, CL and sphere movements combine in endless permutations to produce an infinite number of integrated torso movements while maintaining maximum awareness and stability. In the next chapter we will present a number of CL and sphere movement combinations as seed movements for the purposes of acquiring and using strength.

CL and sphere movements combine in endless permutations to produce an infinite number of integrated torso movements while maintaining maximum awareness and stability.

Chapter 8

Building Strength with Awareness

1. Discovering the Pulse of Life

For the first few years, I was pretty macho in my standing practice. Not understanding the true purpose of the practice, I approached it in a traditional western manner as a contest of strength and endurance. I thought the idea was to hold and maintain the positions with a lot of strength, and for as long as possible, often standing for more than an hour, sometimes twice or three times a day. I know now that I was only holding onto, and in fact creating, a lot of tension.

Always a late bloomer, it was not until my third year of standing meditation that I had a breakthrough experience. Three very small movements occurred simultaneously, producing a profound realization, a revelation that crystallized my basic understanding of the essence of the art of Yiquan.

The experience was that of song, usually translated as the state of being relaxed or the act of relaxing. It is important to realize in this context that the idea of song as relaxation and letting go of tension does not connote a state of physical collapse and diminished consciousness. On the contrary, song connotes a state of stillness with heightened alertness and readiness for action, much like a cat when it is ready to pounce.

I was holding the universal posture in a lowered stance, near the point of exhaustion, and feeling like I was about to collapse physically. My body had shaken and quivered until it had no strength left. And because it had no strength left, my body had no resistance left to the inherent power of the posture I was holding to achieve the most economical structure. All the residual tensions that I was still holding relaxed at the same time and released in one prolonged involuntary sigh.

As I sighed, my hips released physically and my torso and CL spontaneously sank just a bit; my coccyx naturally pulled under, and as the pelvis tilted forward and up, the lumbar curve disappeared as I felt my spine straighten and lengthen.

Simultaneously the release of tension allowed me to fully sink my weight through my legs into my feet, and to root my torso into the ground in a way I had never experienced before.

The musculature involved in the sphere made by my arms and upper body also released their accumulated tension and naturally expanded equally in all directions.

All in all, I felt as though I was a balloon that, because someone was pushing down upon it, was expanding equally in all directions. Each of these three movements was very small in itself, but experientially they were highly significant because they were the physical manifestations of my body settling into its oneness of strength and structure.

Up to this point, I had been performing the movement exercises mechanically, without understanding why I was doing what I was doing, acting on faith that eventually

146

Chapter 8 Building Strength with Awareness

something would happen and the insight would come. In the months and years that followed, many realizations flowed from this experience and slowly coalesced into a conceptual understanding of the Yiquan system's "method of cultivating strength" (shili) and "method of using strength" (fali) for self defense and martial arts.

After that initial experience of the high of song, I naturally wanted more. Subsequent experimentation in recreating the sensations convinced me that the shili component of Yiquan practice allowed one to access and gain control over the basic pulse of life itself. By deeply understanding the relationship between the inhalation-exhalation cycle of the breath and the polarity of tension and relaxation, one begins to experience the fundamental charge and discharge cycle that moves life.

In this polarity, exhalation, as I described in my experience above, is associated with relaxation and discharge, and is therefore yin. Conversely, inhalation is yang because it is associated with holding tension or charge, which, as discussed before, manifests in everyday breathing pathologies and deformed postural patterns in most people.

As described by Wilhelm Reich and other biologists, the fundamental characteristic of life is the pulsatory cycle of charge and discharge of organismic energy. This can be observed in its purest and most primeval form in the spherical structure of the single cell. Plasmatic streamings from the center of the cellular sphere to its periphery and back occur in a rhythmic pulse of contraction-expansion, of charge and discharge, of tension (gathering) and relaxation (release) of energy.[1]

The pulse of relaxation and letting go I felt as I exhaled in my song experience originated in my wuji or center point. This is the gravitational and biological center located in the abdomen midway between the dantien in the front and mingmen in the back. From there the euphoric wave of release spread to my extremities, suffusing torso, legs, feet, arms and hands. Working with the breath as the primary pulsation of life, I began to systematically cultivate experiencing the direction of charge or energy flow from periphery to center on the inhale and from center to periphery on the exhale.

2. Breathing for relaxation and strength

Yiquan synthesized Buddhist, Taoist, and Confucian breathing and sound methods as part of Yiquan, supplementing the practice of shili: "Owing to congenital reasons, physiological structure varies with different people. Each exerciser therefore has his own special points in the body which are not easily accessible by strength… [Therefore] the function of the trial of breath is to activate all the cells in the body with sound waves"[2] in order to functionally integrate all the body's parts.

The purpose of conscious breathing practice in Yiquan is to facilitate the integration of the upper and lower halves of the torso, as well as the integration of the torso as a whole with its foundation and sphere. The method is the exaggerated use of fundamental spinal mechanics associated with the inhalation-exhalation cycle of the breath.

In a natural breath cycle, which includes the charge and discharge of energy, a naturally strong and flexible

Chapter 8 Building Strength with Awareness

spine functions as follows. On the inhale, or charging part of the cycle, the top and bottom tips of the spine will naturally arc backward a little, creating a convex spinal and torso curve, with the head tilted back and up slightly and the tail bone and buttocks also sticking out. On the exhale, or discharging part of the cycle, the converse happens, the pelvis and tail bone naturally pulling forward and up in what is usually called the "pelvic tilt." The head also inclines forward a little, and the chin is naturally pulled in somewhat. These two actions combine to straighten and lengthen the vertical alignment of the spine.

In harmonizing the breath with the shili movements, the main emphasis should be on the integrative function of the exhalation. On every exhale, exert and exaggerate the pulling and tilting of the pelvis and chin, as if pulling the tailbone and chin towards each other. On every inhale, have no intention or exertion; simply allow the head and tail to move naturally, tilting backward a little.

Pay attention to how the tucking of the tailbone by means of the pelvic tilt initiates a wave of energy up through the lumbar and thoracic curves of the spine. The tucking of the chin prevents the dissipation of the energy wave upward and out the top of the spine and head, redirecting it to fill and expand the sphere of the arms. Thus, on every exhalation, the torso as a whole exerts and is filled with a tension that stretches all muscles, ligaments and tendons of the body equally within the structure of whatever shili posture or movement is being worked with. Conversely, on every inhale, we do not exert, and feel the body emptied of tension.

Over time this practice led to an even deeper understanding of the inter-penetration of yin and yang in the Yiquan exercises. As I progressed and my body became more and more song during exhalation, I discovered a new kind of strength. The elastic expansion of my entire being resulted in an integration and unification of my body's three springs I had never before experienced.

As a result I began working with conscious use of tension in the relaxation phase of the breathing cycle, filling my body with tension during exhalation. Conversely, I also began to use conscious relaxation during the tension phase of the breath, emptying my body of tension during the inhalation. These uses of tension within relaxation and relaxation within tension have allowed me, over the years, to development a small measure of the truly integrated, yet elastic, strength characteristic of the Yiquan adept.

> I began working with conscious use of tension in the relaxation phase of the breathing cycle, filling my body with tension during exhalation. Conversely, I also began to use conscious relaxation during the tension phase of the breath, emptying my body of tension during the inhalation.

3. Pulse Energy Exercises

The eight postures Han Sifu taught us represent different polarity aspects of the universal sphere. The rotational polarity features prominently. The only difference between postures #1 and #2, #3 and #4, and #6 and #7 is the forearm rotation. Likewise, the vertical polarity: #1 and #2 are medium high and #2 and #4 are medium low; #5 is very high and #8 is very low; #6 and #7 are extended as opposed to #1 and #2, which are retracted.

The following shili pulse exercises integrate the movement of the CL of the torso (carried out by the foundation of the legs) with the sphere of the arms.

Chapter 8 Building Strength with Awareness

Awareness exercise 8-1. Begin with standing in Master Han's #1 posture. In the pulse with simple horizontal circle, the breathing cycle harmonizes with the sphere polarities of extension-retraction and opening-closing. On the inhale, raise the CL while retracting and opening the sphere. On the exhale, lower the CL, extend and close the sphere. This allows the hands to make two horizontal circles in front of their respective shoulders. Don't make the movements too big.

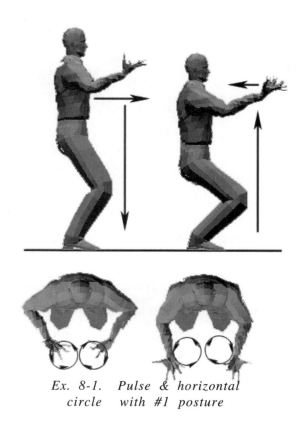

Ex. 8-1.   Pulse & horizontal circle   with #1 posture

Awareness exercise 8-2. Do the same with Master Han's posture #2.

Awareness exercise 8-3. Now add the rotation of the forearms, as follows. On the inhale, as the arms retract and open, the forearms rotate to #1 position. On the exhale, as the arms begin to extend and open, rotate the forearms into #2 position. Imagine pulling something towards you on the inhale and pushing something away on the exhale.

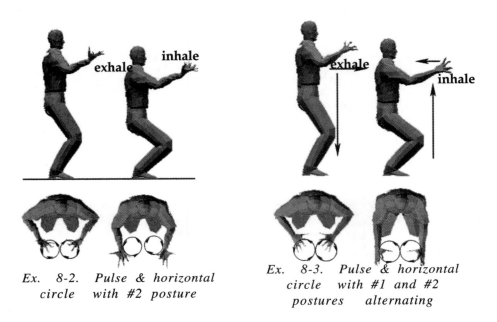

Ex. 8-2. Pulse & horizontal circle with #2 posture

Ex. 8-3. Pulse & horizontal circle with #1 and #2 postures alternating

Awareness exercise 8-4. Note that the default method of making the sphere of the arms contract and expand is to use the elbows as a fulcrum point (A). This means there is even expansion of the sphere forward (with hands) and backward (with the shoulders). Feel the difference when you use either the hands (C) or shoulders (B) as the fulcrum points by keeping them steady. When the shoulders are fixed, the only expansion is forward; when the hands are fixed, the only expansion is backward.

Awareness exercise 8-5. When we add the up-down polarity of the arms to the fundamental action of extending-retracting, we obtain the vertical circle pulse. The vertical circle of the arms harmonizes naturally with the pulse of the breath and CL movements. From #1 posture

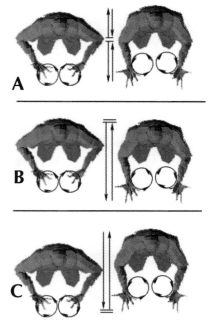

*Ex. 8-4. Using elbows (A), shoulders (B),
and hands (C) as fulcrum*

(A), as you exhale, lower the torso and CL and extend the
arms to #6 posture (B), and further sink and lower the arms
to #3 posture (C). On the inhale, raise torso and arms to #1
posture. Also do with arms rotated and palms down (#2
posture.

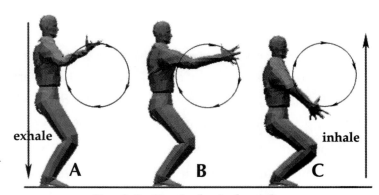

Ex. 8-5. Vertical circle pulse

Awareness exercise 8-6. Reverse the direction of
movement: On exhale, sink the CL and lower the arms to
#3 posture (B). On the inhale, raise the CL,and extend the

153

arms to #6 posture (C). Also practice with forearms rotated with palms down to #2 posture.

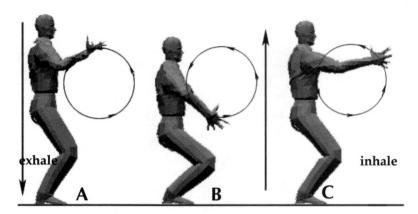

Ex. 8-6. Vertical circle pulse (2)

Awareness exercise 8-7. Experiment and add the rotation of the forearms while making the various vertical circles. For example, in awareness exercise 8-5, rotate forearms to #2 position before extending to #6.

4. Wave Energy Exercises

The waveform of biological energy is more complex than the simple pulsation of the cellular sphere. It appears on the evolutionary ladder with directionality, with polarization along an axis of orientation with head and tail, which henceforth defines movement as forward-backward. The unicellular sphere elongates and differentiates into tubular, cylindrical structures, with movement typical to that of worms and snakes, in which locomotion is produced by energy waves that travel rhythmically from tail to front.

Chapter 8 Building Strength with Awareness

The wave is what is referred to in the classic saying that "energy begins in the feet...and is expressed in the hands." Wave energy is generated in the practice of shili with a coordination of breath with the action of the foundation spring reversed from that used in the production of pulse. As you exhale, you sequentially extend the body's three springs—first the foundation, then the torso, and finally then the sphere. Conversely, as you inhale, you bring the energy from the hands/arms down the torso, into the foundation by the sequential flexing of the spring. Thus all the previous pulse exercises are transformed into wave exercises.

Awareness exercise 8-8. Begin with standing in Master Han's #1 posture. In the wave with simple horizontal circle, the breathing cycle harmonizes with the sphere polarities of extension-retraction and opening-closing. On the inhale, lower the CL while retracting and opening the sphere. On the exhale, raise the CL, extend and close the sphere. This allows the hands to make two horizontal circles in front of their respective shoulders. Don't make the movements too big.

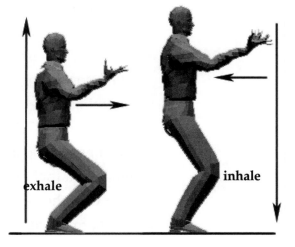

Awareness exercise 8-9. Do the same with Master Han's posture #2.

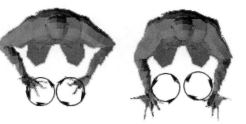

Ex. 8-8. Wave with horizontal circle in #1 posture

155

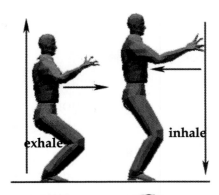
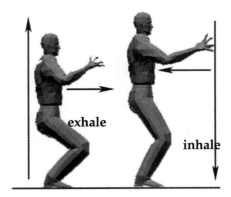

Ex. 8-9. Wave with horizontal circle in #2 posture

Ex. 8-10. Wave with horizontal circle and alternating #1-#2

Awareness exercise 8-10. Now add the rotation of the forearms, as follows. On the inhale, lower the CL as the arms retract and open; the forearms rotate to #1 position. On the exhale, raise the CL as the arms begin to extend and open; rotate the forearms into #2 position. Imagine pulling something towards you on the inhale and pushing something away on the exhale.

When we add the up-down polarity of the arms to the fundamental action of extending-retracting, we obtain the wave with the vertical circle . The vertical circle of the arms harmonizes naturally with the wave of the breath and CL movements.

Awareness exercise 8-11. From #1 posture (A), as you inhale, lower the torso and CL and extend the arms to #6 posture (B), and further sink and lower the arms to #3 posture (C). On the exhale, raise torso and arms to #1

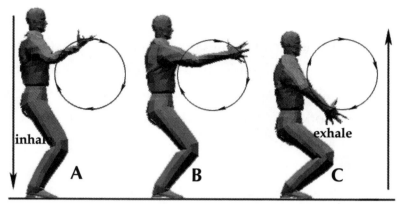

Ex. 8-11. Wave with vertical circle in #1 posture

posture (A). Also do with arms rotated and palms down in #2 posture.

Awareness exercise 8-12. Reverse the direction of movement: Start with #1 posture (A). On inhale, lower the CL and the arms to #3 posture (B). On the exhale, raise the CL,and extend the arms to #6 posture (C). Also practice with forearms rotated with palms down to #2 posture.

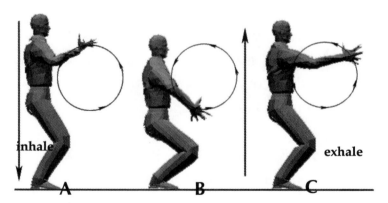

Ex. 8-12. Wave with vertical circle in #1 posture

5. Further Wave Exercises

The structure and orientation of the body in space creates two possible kinds of CL shifting: front-back and left-right. In the parallel stance, the shifting in the front-back direction can occur only from the balls to the heels of both feet simultaneously (instead of from foot to foot as in the archer stance). This can clearly be experienced when working with the horizontal and vertical circles described above.

In fact, one way of practicing when making these circles is to attempt NOT to shift back and forth from the heels to balls of the feet and limit the CL movement to ONLY up-down. As you do this try making the elbows the center joint of the spring of the arms. With the elbows fixed as the fulcrum, the action of extending the arms results in the equal expansion of the sphere with the hands going forward and the back going backwards.

Shifting the CL in parallel stance, therefore, is necessarily mostly from left to right. Corresponding to the alternation of weight between the feet, there is an alternation of the up-down movement of the hands. The hand in which the energy is expressed rises and the other lowers and is used to counteract and stabilize downward the upward thrust of the lifting one

Awareness exercise 8-13. Start with Master Han's posture #7 (A). Shift the CL and weight onto the left foot. Pushing from the left foot, shift the CL to the right foot, as the right hand simultaneously rises (B). Then as you shift left, the left hand rises as the right hand lowers (C), etc. Let the hands make straight lines up down in front of the body/ shoulders.

Ex. 8-13. Shifting with alternate

Awareness exercise 8-14. Imagine these two vertical lines as the diameters of two circles. Then trace the circles with the hands, harmonizing with the shifting and up-down CL movement. Pushing off from the left foot and shifting right, the right hand will come up the front middle of the body in a semi-circular fashion; it will descend in a semicircle on the right outside of the body. When shifting back to the left, the left hand traces its circle and goes up the front of the body towards the left outside. The hands now are also making alternating circles that together make a figure 8.

Ex. 8-14. Shifting with alternating circles

Awareness exercise 8-15. Now go back to making straight lines, but reverse the up-down movement of the arms relative to the shifting. When shifting to the left foot raise the right arm and lower the left (B). Likewise when shifting to the right foot, raise the left arm and lower the right (C).

Awareness exercise 8-16. Again, imagine straight lines to be the diameters of two circles, and trace the cicles as illustrated in *Ex.8-16*. This is the opposite direction from *Ex.8-14*.

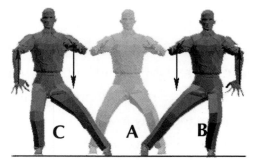

Ex. 8-15. Shifting with reverse alternate raising and lowering of arms

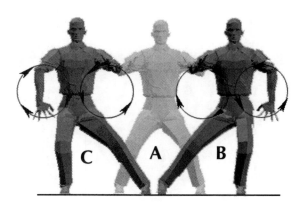

Ex. 8-16. Shifting with reverse alternate circling of arms

Chapter 8 Building Strength with Awareness

When this CL shifting is combined with CL up-down movement, the essential waveform of the energy becomes even clearer. To feel this, at first disregard the hands, shifting simply from left to right. Once on the right, lower the CL a little. Then when you shift left, simultaneously push up and raise the CL. Then while on the left, lower it again before shifting to the right and raising it.

Now add the various up-down and circling of the hands back into this combined CL movement pattern. In all this shifting back and forth, take scrupulous care to keep your weight even between the inside and outside of both feet.

6. Spiral Energy Exercises

The third basic form of biological energy is spiral energy. The energetic structure of spiral energy is rotational action of the biological cylinder added to the wave, propagated along the longitudinal axis of the organism. Yiquan's strength-building shili exercises utilize rotation of the springs of the body to create the specifically human spiral energy force. Thus, in addition to the retraction-extension forces generated by the action of the three springs, there is added the torsion forces of rotation of the foundation, torso and sphere.

The energetic structure of spiral energy is rotational action of the biological cylinder added to the wave, propagated along the longitudinal axis of the organism.

The rotational ability of the torso and CL derives from the functional structure of the hips that allows the legs as a cylindrical unit to rotate along its longitudinal axis clockwise and counterclockwise.

The toeing out of the foot and eversion, or turning out, of the leg generally works with the retraction of the leg to

161

receive and root energy by sinking and opening at the hip. The toeing in, and inversion (turning in) of the leg generally works with the extension of the leg to issue or discharge energy, by raising the torso and closing at the hip.

Awareness exercise 8-18. Stand in the parallel stance (A) and alternately turn the toes of both feet out (B) and in (C) . With toes turned out (B), you will be able to sink and root the CL significantly better than in the parallel stance (A). With toes turned in, you will not be able to sink the torso and the CL as low as in the parallel stance, let alone the everted stance.

Ex. 8-18. Effect of rotating the legs on raising and lowering of the torso

In shili, these two abilities work together by simultaneously opposing each other, and in doing so creating a stable base that allows the effortless rotation of the torso on the hips.

Awareness exercise 8-19. In the parallel stance, begin by expanding the knees outward, as if there is an

162

expanding balloon between them. This puts the weight on the outside of the feet. Then restrain that expansion by equalizing the distribution of the weight between the inside and the outside of the foot. This will stabilize and fix the knees above the feet and will create an isometric state of dynamic stillness and stability of the base, which will allow for effortless rotation of the torso on the hip joints.

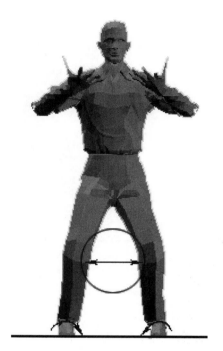

Ex. 8-19.
Stabilizing the foundation

Now that we know how to rotate the CL and torso while keeping a stable base, let's add the hands, making a number of basic rotational circles, to complete the generation and expression of spiral energy patterns. Begin by observing the fundamental harmony of the rotational movement of the centerline with inverson-eversion rotation of the arms in this simple pulling-pushing exercise.

Awareness exercise 8-20. In parallel stance allow the rotation of the CL to dictate corresponding rotation in the forearms, resulting in the alternate and opposing change in hands from #1 to #2 posture as the CL rotates clockwise-counterclockwise. When you turn to the left, your right palm is up in #1 posture and left palm down in #2 posture (B) and vice versa (C). Notice that the hips, shoulders, and palms rotate from diagonal to diagonal as a unit. Also do the reverse: turn to the left with right palm down and left palm up, and turn to the right with left palm down and right palm up.

Ex. 8-20. Harmonizing the rotation of the forearms with the CL and torso

Awareness exercise 8-21. Now add more of a pulling-pushing sensation, emphasizing that the movement is led from and originates in the hip that is pulling back. You must feel that pulling back the arm produces the rotational, screwing in like forward movement of the opposing arm. Note that the head does not rotate with body, and the intent is straight ahead, not diagonal.

Ex. 8-21. Spiralling energy in and out with rotation of CL and forearms.

Awareness exercise 8-22. Then elevate one arm to the level of the ear and imagine you're holding a giant ball that you turn over and back as you are rotating the body from one side to the other. This might be experienced as similar to doing the forward crawl in swimming, motivated by the rotation of the CL and torso.

Ex. 8-22. Circling and rotating the arms and torso as if swimming in the forward crawl.

Awareness exercise 8-23. Reverse the direction to imitate the backward crawl. Emphasize motion originating in the hip and leading the movement.

Ex. 8-23. Circling and rotating the arms and torso as if swimming in the backward crawl.

Do these same exercises, alternating direction to the left and right corners. Also experiment with adding the raising-lowering and shifting left-right CL movements.

Likewise experiment with the oppositional movements of the arms, as in *Ex.8-24.*

Awareness exercise 8-24. With your center low over the right foot (A), raise , rotate and shift the CL to high over the left foot(B). Simultaneously raise and lower arms alternately from high #1 or #6 to low #4 with simultaneous rotation of forearms, as in "wild horse parting mane," or "cloudhands." Then lower CL over (B), and shift, raise and rotate to high (A), with corresponding movement of the arms.

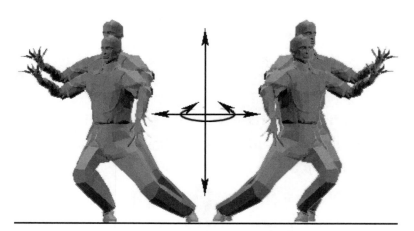

Ex. 8-24. Combining CL movements with alternating arm movements

7. Functional Stances & Movement

In zhanzhuang, any and all of the eight postures held in the parallel stance can be held in the functional stance. For the sake of convenience, we identify and use the following three postures, fully understanding that any position between the extremes can be used: (1) weight 100% on rear foot; (2) small and high stance with weight

Chapter 8 Building Strength with Awareness

70% on rear foot, 30% on front; (3) weight distributed 50/50 in "large low archer stance," to borrow a phrase from Taiji.

All of the pulse, wave, and spiral exercises done in the parallel stance should also be practiced in the functional stances, other than the CL shifting exercises which are, by definition, eliminated in the 100% rear-weighted stances. Pulse, wave and spiral exercises in the archer stances lead to interesting discoveries.

Awareness exercise 8-25. Begin by doing the pulse of the horizontal circle. Maintain the weight 50/50 while sinking the CL and extending the torso spring by tucking tail and chin and extending the sphere of the arms. First use #1, then #2 postures, and then alternate between them in pulling (*Ex.8-25 B*) and pushing movements (*Ex.8-25 A*). Fix the elbows as a fulcrum, so that there is equal movement in and out, forward and backward, between hands and shoulders.

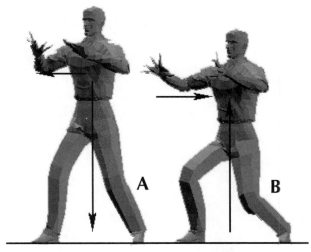

Ex. 8-25. Vertical CL movement in archer stance with expansion and contraction of the sphere

Using the horizontal circle and shifting the CL forward and backward in the archer stance, harmonized with the pulling-pushing action of the sphere, we can generate two opposing variations of the wave form of energy.

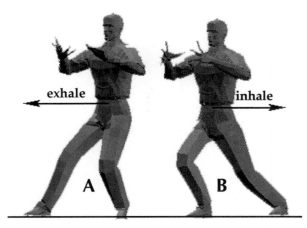

Ex. 8-26. Horizontal CL movement in archer stance with expansion and contraction of the sphere

Awareness exercise 8-26. As you inhale and shift back, rotate the palms towards you and flex the arms as if pulling something towards you *(Ex.8-26A)*. As you shift forward and exhale, rotate the palms out and extend the arms, as if pushing something away and forward *(Ex.8-26B)*. In this exercise the wave originates in the rear foot and is expressed in the forward thrust of torso and hands.

Awareness exercise 8-27. Now fix the hands and don't let them move as you retract and extend the arms. As you inhale and flex, you will pull yourself forward and shift the CL to the front foot *(Ex.8-27A)*. As you exhale, you will push your torso and shift the CL backward to the rear foot *(Ex.8-27B)*, as if pushing something backward with your shoulders. In this exercise, the wave originates in the front foot and is expressed in the backward thrust of the shoulders.

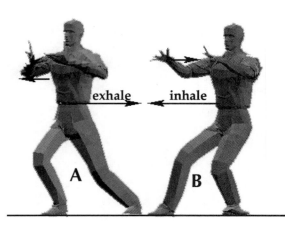

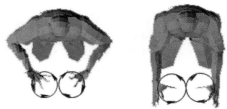

Ex. 8-27. Horizontal CL movement in archer stance with reverse expansion and contraction of the sphere

Lowering and raising the CL can be added to emphasize the waveform while making the vertical circle with the torso.

Chapter 8 Building Strength with Awareness

Awareness exercise 8-28. Sink the CL on the rear foot on the inhale *(Ex.8-28B)* before shifting forward and raising it on the exhale *(Ex.8-28A)*, pushing forward and up with the hands.

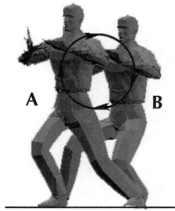

Ex. 8-28. Making verticle circles with torso

Awareness exercise 8-29. Sink the CL on the front foot on the inhale *(Ex.8-29A)* before shifting backward and raising it on the exhale *(Ex.8-29B)*, pushing back and up with the shoulders.

Awareness exercise 8-30. Add the arms to the vertical circle. As you inhale, shift back and retract the sphere to chest level, then sink the CL and lower the sphere. On the exhale, raise the sphere as you shift the CL forward. Use #1 and # 2 positions separately, then alternate.

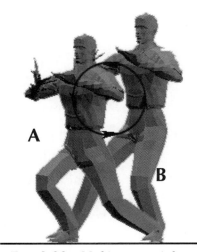

Ex. 8-29. Making verticle circles with torso

Awareness exercise 8-31. Reverse direction. As you inhale and shift back, lower the sphere, as if pulling something towards the hips. On the exhale, raise the sphere close to the body as you raise the CL, and expand the sphere forward as you shift the CL forward. Use #1 and # 2 positions separately, then alternate.

Likewise practice all the variations of the alternating and rotational circles

Ex. 8-30. Vertical circling of torso and arms

Ex. 8-31. Reverse vertical circling of torso and arms

described previously for parallel stance in the functional stances. Notice the differences you experience in the same CL and sphere movements done in parallel and functional stances. Remember that this is Yiquan, the system of the mind. Therefore, in order to discover the interplay between attention and intention, you must experiment and make up different permutations and combinations using the grammar of movement for the CL and the sphere.

8. Walking Movement Exercises

Do every shili pulse, wave, and spiral awareness exercise while walking—especially horizontal and vertical, alternating and rotational circles.

Awareness exercise 8-32. In walking forward while making horizontal circles (*Ex.8-32*). On the inhale (A) place your right foot in front and contract your sphere. Then on the exhale, shift the CL and expand the sphere (B). Next, on the inhale (C), place your left foot in front and contract your sphere, while on the exhale, shift the CL onto the front left foot and expand the sphere (D).

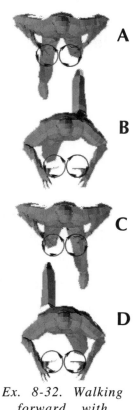

A

B

C

D

Ex. 8-32. Walking forward with horizontal circle

Chapter 8 Building Strength with Awareness

Awareness exercise 8-33. Walking backward while making horizontal circles. In *Ex.8-33*, on the inhale place your left foot in back and contract your sphere (A), while on the exhale, you shift the CL back and expand the sphere (B). On the next inhale, place your right foot to the back and contract your sphere (C), while on the exhale, you shift the CL back again and expand the sphere (D).

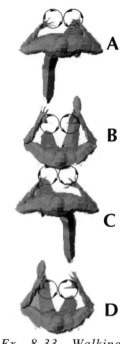

Ex. 8-33. Walking backward with horizontal cicle

Awareness exercise 8-34. Walking forward with the vertical circle. Begin with CL on rear left foot and hands in posture #3 *(Ex.8-34A)*. Inhale. As you exhale, shift forward to the right foot and circle the arms towards the body, up and forward *(Ex.8-34B)*. As you inhale place the left foot in front and circle the arms down *(Ex.8-34C)*. Then as you exhale, shift the CL forward to the left foot and circle the arms up and out to # 2 or # 6 posture, depending on the size of the circle. First do this execise with forearms turned one way, then the other, then alternate them as shown in *Ex.8-34.*

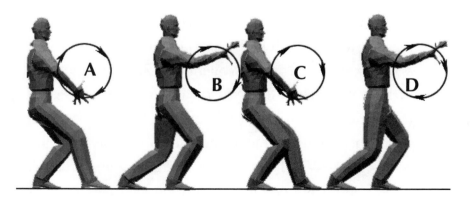

Ex. 8-34. Walking forward with the vertical circle

Awareness exercise 8-35. Now reverse the direction of the circle of the arms. Begin with CL on rear left foot and hands in posture #3 *(Ex.8-35A)*. Inhale. As you exhale, shift forward to the right foot and circle the arms away from the body up and forward *(Ex.8-35B)*. As you inhale, place the left foot in front and circle the arms down *(Ex.8-35C)*. Then as you exhale, shift the CL forward to the left foot and circle the arms up and out to # 2 or # 6 posture, depending on the size of the circle. First do with forearms turned one way, then the other, then alternate them as shown in *Ex.8-35*.

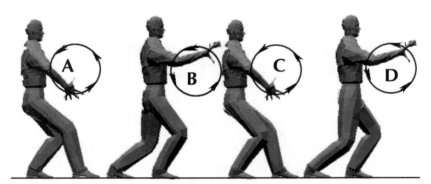

Ex. 8-35. Walking forward with the reverse vertical circle

Awareness exercise 8-36. Walking backward with the vertical circle. Start with CL on front right foot *(Ex.8-36A)*. Inhale. As you exhale, shift the CL backwards to the rear left foot and circle the arms up and away from the body *(Ex.8-36B)*. Then, as you inhale, place the right foot to the rear and circle the arms towards the body and down *(Ex.8-36C)*. As you exhale, shift the CL backwards to the rear right foot and circle the arms up and away from the body *(Ex.8-36D)*. First do this exercise with forearms turned one way, then the other, then alternate them as shown in *Ex.8-36*.

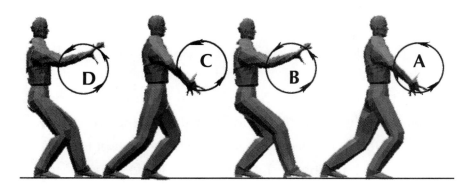

Ex. 8-36. Walking backward with the vertical circle

Awareness exercise 8-37. Now walk backward reversing the circle of the arms. Start with CL on front right foot *(Ex.8-37A)*. Inhale. As you exhale, shift the CL backwards to the rear left foot and circle the arms first up and towards, and then away from the body *(Ex.8-37B)*. Then, as you inhale, place the right foot to the rear and circle the arms away from the body and down *(Ex.8-37C)*. As you exhale, shift the CL backwards to the rear right foot and circle the arms up and away from the body *(Ex.8-37D)*. First do with forearms turned one way, then the other, then alternate them as shown in *Ex.8-37*.

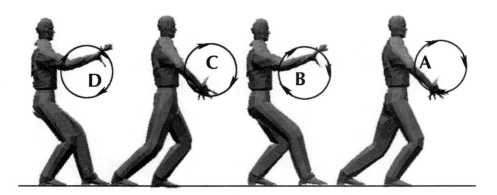

Ex. 8-37. Walking backward with the   reversevertical circle

Awareness exercise 8-38. Walking forward with alternating circles. Start with CL on front left leg, left hand high and right hand low *(Ex.8-38A)*. Inhale and place the right foot in front. As you exhale, the CL shifts to the front right foot and the right hand circles up in front of the body while the left hand circles down on the outside of the body *(Ex.8-38B)*. Then inhale as you place the left foot in front. As you exhale, the CL shifts to the front left foot and the left hand circles up in front of the body while the right hand circles down on the outside of the body *(Ex.8-38A)*. Also do this exercise while reversing the direction of the circle of the arms.

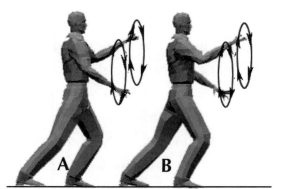

Ex. 8-38. Walking forward with alternating circles

Awareness exercise 8-39. In walking backward with alternating circles, start with CL on rear left leg, left hand low and right hand high *(Ex.8-39A)*. Inhale and place the right foot to the rear. As you exhale, the CL shifts to the rear right foot and the right hand circles down in front of the body while the left hand circles up on the outside of the body *(Ex.8-39B)*. Then inhale as you place the left foot in the rear. As you exhale, the CL shifts to the rear left foot and the right hand circles up in front of the body while the left hand circles down on the outside of the body *(Ex.8-36A)*. Also do the exercise reversing the direction of the circle of the arms.

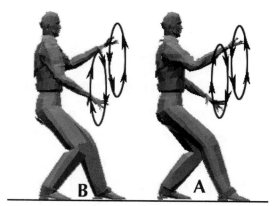

Ex. 8-39.   Walking backward with alternating circles

Awareness exercise 8-40. Start with CL on front left foot. Torso is rotated to left corner. Right hand in #1 posture spiralling forward, left hand in #2 posture spiralling backward *(Ex.8-40A)*. As you inhale, place the right foot in front. As you exhale, shift the CL to front right foot, rotate torso to right corner, and rotate the forearms so the left hand is spiralling forward in #1 posture and right hand

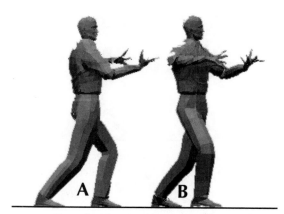

Ex. 8-40. Walking forward with CL and forearm rotation

is "un"spiralling backward in #2 posture *(Ex.8-340B)*. As you inhale, place the left foot in front. As you exhale, shift the CL forward to left foot, rotate torso to the left corner, and rotate right hand to #1 posture spiralling forward, and rotate left hand in #2 posture spiralling backward *(Ex.8-40A)*.

Awareness exercise 8-41. Start with CL on rear right foot. Torso is rotated to left corner. Right hand in #1 posture spiralling forward, left hand in #2 posture spiralling backward *(Ex.8-41A)*. As you inhale, place the left foot to rear. As you exhale, shift the CL to rear left foot, rotate torso to right corner, and rotate the forearms so the left hand is spiralling forward in #1 posture and right hand is spiralling backward in #2 posture *(Ex.8-41B)*. As you inhale, place the right foot in rear. As you exhale, shift the CL backward to left foot, rotate torso to the left corner, and rotate right hand to #1 posture spiralling forward, and rotate left hand in #2 posture spiralling backward *(Ex.8-41A)*.

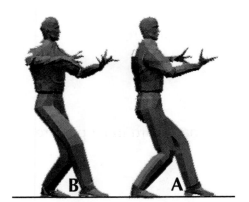

Ex. 8-41. Walking backward with CL and forearm rotation

Chapter 8 Building Strength with Awareness

Awareness exercise 8-42. Walking forward with CL rotation and turning the sphere. Start with CL on front left foot. Torso is rotated to left corner. Right hand low in #1 posture spiralling forward, left hand high in #2 posture spiralling backward *(Ex.8-42A)*. As you inhale, place the right foot in front. As you exhale, shift the CL to front right foot, rotate torso to right corner, and rotate the forearms so the left hand lowers, spiralling forward in #1 posture and right hand raises, spiralling backward in #2 posture *(Ex.8-42B)*. As you inhale, place the

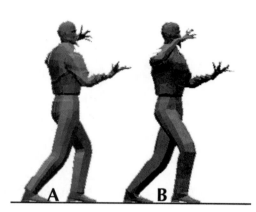

Ex. 8-42. Walking forward with CL rotation and turning the sphere

left foot in front. As you exhale, shift the CL forward to left foot, rotate torso to the left corner, lower and rotate right hand to #1 posture spiralling forward, and raise and rotate left hand in #2 posture spiralling backward *(Ex.8-42A)*.

Awareness exercise 8-43. Start with CL on rear right foot. Torso is rotated to left corner. Right hand in #1 posture spiralling forward, left hand in #2 posture spiralling backward *(Ex.8-43A)*. As you inhale, place the left foot to rear. As you exhale, shift the CL to rear left foot, rotate torso to right corner, and rotate the forearms so the left hand is spiralling forward in #1 posture and right hand is spiralling backward in #2 posture *(Ex.8-43B)*. As you inhale, place the right foot in rear. As you exhale, shift the CL backward to left foot, rotate torso to the left corner, and rotate right hand to #1 posture spiralling forward, and rotate left hand in #2 posture spiralling backward *(Ex.8-43A)*.

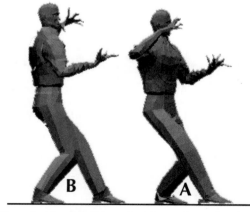

Ex. 8-43. Walking backward with CL rotation and turning the sphere

9. The Use of Sound

The use of sound is derived from, and an adjunct to, the use of breath in the meditative and martial arts, and has been explored since time immemorial. Generally, it was found that the practice of certain sounds, as part of the discipline, produced certain predictable and desirable results, both for health and martial arts uses. Generally, to promote health and harmony the practice of vowel sounds is used, whereas for martial arts purposes, consonant fricatives or stops are used.

Probably the most ancient and universal of all sound practices is the use of the sound "Om," or "aum," the vibrations of which engender in the practitioner a feeling of ecstasy and harmony with the universe. Likewise in the more complicated mantras, the practitioner, through the prolonged repetition of certain sounds or phrases, stills the mind of thought and thereby allows it to enter into higher realms of awareness.[3] In traditional Taoist practice there is the discipline of the "six healing sounds," in which a different sound is produced and practiced to heal and harmonize the function of each major organ—kidneys, spleen, heart, liver, lungs, and triple warmer.[4]

In the practice of the Taijiquan system of health and self-defense the "heng" and "ha" sounds are utilized in harmony with the inhalation and exhalation of the breath to promote internal strength[5]. In Karate and many other Kung Fu systems, explosive utterances are utilized to accompany and increase the discharge of energy in punches and kicks.

Chapter 8 Building Strength with Awareness

Modern anatomical and physiological science has clarified both the function and the physiological mechanisms of sound production in health and martial arts. Expiratory aspirates and sibilants in particular have been shown to be human analogs to primitive mammalian defense mechanisms in which the entire body is marshaled for emergency service. These sounds integrate the body, engaging the lower trunk's flight or fight musculature for immediate and concerted action. Breathing, postural, and locomotive rhythms are harmonized while lowering the center of gravity in anticipation of immediate powerful action[6].

In my own practice of sound in shili exercises, therefore, I have adopted the sound made during the "green dragon turns its head" exercise of the ancient Yijinjing series in which, during the exhalation, the air is expelled forcibly by hissing through the teeth. The Yijinjing practice is actually within the Yiquan tradition, since Wang Xiangzhai considered both to ultimately have derived from the same Buddhist root, namely Bodhidharma's system of health and self defense.[7]

Wang Xuan Jie describes the primary sound to be used in shili as "ha" or "ah." Wang Xuan Jie also describes the training and perfection of sound as "inner breathing" or "back-breathing," an exercise that starts with the locus of sound production being the mouth. In terms of the ancient mammalian sound patterns described above, note that the "h" sound is most nearly like the low guttural growl or the hiss of the alarmed animal."[8]

The sound made is systematically internalized by "the skills of internal transformation." First it is lowered into the chest, then moved into the back of the throat, and finally it is sunk into the lower abdomen (dantien). As this process unfolds in the practitioner, the sound quality gradually goes from audible to inaudible. As the sound production moves to the abdomen and becomes inaudible, the sound is transformed into breath, or energy (qi), at which time "sound and strength are produced simultaneously."[9]

Chapter 9

Using Strength with Awareness

1. The Internalization of Movement

As mentioned earlier regarding the range movement of the body, Wang Xiangzhai said that "small movement is better than big movement and no movement is better than small movement." Any conscious movement, large or small, is produced by an intention. Therefore, going from large to small to no movement with identical intention is going from the physical to the mental or purely intentional realm: hence Yiquan.

In our practice we use the simple but profound technique of internalization of movement to develop the ability for purely intentional movement. Do any and all shili movements a number of times, and each successive time you do it, make the movement a little smaller, gradually making the movements so small that there is no longer any visible external movement. Yet on the inside you continue to have the sensation of the movement.

Use the simple but profound technique of internalization of movement to develop the ability for purely intentional movement.

Thus intentional movement is defined as the internal sensation of movement without any visible expression being produced by the mind's intention. In this state, the body moving in circles becomes circles moving in the body; the energy of the body's movement becomes the movement of energy throughout the body.

2. Awareness exercises

As with shili exercises, when practicing intentional movements, always proceed from the simple to the complex and from the sequential to the simultaneous. Regarding centerline (CL) movements, for example, first practice internalizing the elemental and most basic patterns of up-down, shifting, and rotational movements separately and repeatedly in order to establish the pathways of neurological habit and kinesthetic awareness. Only then practice internalizing sequential combinations and finally simultaneous combinations.

> **When practicing intentional movements, always proceed from the simple to the complex and from the sequential to the simultaneous.**

The intentional movements of the sphere are similar in essence to those of the CL, except that the mathematical possibilities here are even greater as a result of the fact that we are working with four, rather than three, polarity structures interacting in combinations. The procedure of internalization is the same.

Start by internalizing the simple movements of (1) extending-retracting, (2) raising-lowering (3) opening-closing, and (4) everting-inverting. Then combine them into the horizontal, vertical, alternating, and rotational circles with appropriate movements of the CL, thus internalizing all possible pulses, waves and spirals.

3. Internal isometrics

Combining the technique of internalizing movements with isometric principles enables the Yiquan artist to transform the slow movements of shili into a dynamic stillness from which the Yi (mind, intent) can explode the elastic strength acquired into an instantaneous and deadly jolt of force. In the Yiquan tradition this is called fali, or "attacking strength," whereas in the Taiji and other traditions it is called fajin, a term indicating the explosive nature of the attack.

As a result of their fundamental polarity structure, all vertical, horizontal and rotational movements imply a changing balance of opposing forces. For example, in horizontal CL movement, while shifting forward in the archer stance, if there were no counterbalancing wave of energy from the front foot to the back, we would fall forward. Likewise in shifting backward, if there were no countervailing force from rear foot to the front of the body, we would fall backward. The same is true for the vertical and rotational movements of the CL and sphere.

With any movement, the amount of isometrics employed can be large or small. The greater the resistance, the slower the movement. When the resistance is equal to the thrust, all movement stops completely as the two opposing forces cancel each other out to create a dynamic stillness. For example, in archer stance with sphere, it is isometrics that create the central stability that in turn allows the unitary expansion at the periphery.

> **When the resistance is equal to the thrust, all movement stops completely as the two opposing forces cancel each other out to create a dynamic stillness.**

When simultaneously shifting the torso forward and backward while expanding the arms forward and the back and shoulders backward, all movements cancel each other out. In the energetic structure of the archer stance, the front leg-to-shoulders force counterbalances the rear leg-to-hand force. Secondly, the rear and front foot power the opposition in the sphere of the arms between the forward intent of the palms and the backward intent of the back and shoulder blades respectively.

The canceling out of opposing forces is not limited to the forward-backward direction, but applies equally to the up-down and rotational dimensions. For example, we have seen that in the pulse, the energy of sinking the CL/torso into the foundation is received by the musculature, turning the leg out and spiraling down the legs in rooting. We have also seen that in the wave, the energy moving down ricochets off the feet and earth to spiral back up the musculature of the legs, turning the leg inward and moves up and out of the expanding sphere of torso and arms. If we now activate both tendencies equally, there will be no visible movement but a simultaneous energetic rooting and discharging of energy down into and up from the foundation.

4. Discharging Energy (Fali)

The practice of internal isometrics, added to the practice of intentional movement, fully charges the resulting stillness with the potential for explosive decompression.

The practice of internal isometrics, added to the practice of intentional movement, fully charges the resulting stillness with the potential for explosive decompression. This is the practice of fali, or actually issuing, or discharging, strength and power. All of the postures and movements applicable to shili are also used in fali. The difference lies in methods and aims.

Shili movement is essentially pulsatory: from one posture to another in a semicircular movement and then back to the original posture in another semicircular movement to complete the circle. Shili movements are done slowly: the release of breath into strength, rooting the

Chapter 9 Using Strength with Awareness

body structure, and integrating its musculature through uniform stretching.

In fali, the first half of this shili cycle is speeded up into an instantaneous, unitary explosion of force outward, while in the second half of the cycle there is an immediate retraction of the arms sphere to the original posture. Wang Xuanjie described a basic fali practice technique:

"First slowly pull your hands back to the front of your breast. Then slowly turn your hands inward and start to push your hands forward. Just at the beginning of the hand pushing movement, suddenly and simultaneously shake your forearms and hands forward like throwing something to the front and with your body ramming forward to a proper extent without losing your balance to assist the internal power emission."[1]

The jin produced in fali focuses the totality of the organism's energetic resources by means of a simple intention, in which the internal movement of energy is manifested externally. The explosive character of the jin produced in fali comes from the body as a whole going instantaneously from a state of extreme relaxation to one of extreme tension and focus. It can be likened to the instantaneous inflation of a balloon or ball with so much pressure that it inflates momentarily into a larger sphere as solid as a bowling ball, resulting in an instantaneous discharge of explosive force, known as "fajin."

This realization in turn sheds a new light of understanding on the practice of shili and its importance. The greater the spectrum from extreme relaxation to extreme tension, the more explosive and deadly the fajin power

> **The explosive character of the jin produced in fali comes from the body as a whole going instantaneously from a state of extreme relaxation to one of extreme tension and focus.**

will be. Since shili creates both tension and relaxation through mindful isometric stretching, we must expand the spectrum of tension-relaxation in shili before we can use it to practice jin, or explosive discharge of energy, in fali.

5. Partnered work with Professor Yu

In 1981, Professor Yu Pen Shi, another one of Wang Xiangzhai's most famous students, moved from his native Shanghai to the San Francisco Bay area. His arrival caused quite a stir in the Bay area martial arts community, and

Fig. 9-1. Prof. and Mme Yu with
top Bay Area teachers: from left to right,
Dr. Lai Yat Ke, Fong Ha, Henry Look & Y.C. Wong

when he began teaching, his classes were enormously large, with many of the area's leading gongfu artists,

Chapter 9 Using Strength with Awareness

teachers, and their students attending. As one of the area's leading Yiquan enthusiasts, it fell to Fong Ha to be Professor Yu's main interpreter at his public classes over the next five years or so. For a while Professor Yu and his wife, Madame Ou Yang, stayed at Fong's Berkeley residence as his guests.

Beginning with his arrival, I studied Yiquan with Professor Yu for almost three years. Basic solo work consisted of chair sitting, zhanzhuang standing in only one posture (low #7) for endless hours, shili work emphasizing the vertical movement with this posture, and simple walking with same.

Although I did not grasp its significance for many years, there was a definite yin-yang structure to the partnered work and practices Professor Yu engaged us in. The yang of his partnered practice involved full-force contact and use of fali jin, while the yin of his partnered practice involved using kung jin or "empty force" across a distance, using only awareness. We will postpone a discussion of the latter until the next chapter, and focus here on a description of the ban-ban exercises—or "bong-bong", as we came to call them—as exemplary of partnered fali practice.

> There was a definite yin-yang structure to the partnered work and practices Professor Yu engaged us in. The yang of his partnered practice involved full-force contact and use of fali jin, while the yin of his partnered practice involved using kung jin or "empty force" across a distance, using only awareness.

The ban-ban exercises essentially involved the use of the horizontal circle of the arms and the vertical circle of the CL to neutralize, redirect, and return the opponent's attacking energy to him, adding the discharge of one's own energy onto it. Person A would stand in a small functional stance with arms in universal stance (#1 posture). Person B, the attacker, starting some 10-15 feet

Fig. 9-2. Prof. Yu demonstrating fali discharge

away, would run full-force towards him, palms outward in front of the shoulders, and attempt to push him over and run through him.

Chapter 9 Using Strength with Awareness

Person A, the defender, would split the incoming energy of the opponent's palms by circling his forearms back and opening, while shifting the CL to the back foot and sinking it, thus rooting himself with the opponent's energy. Having exhausted the intent of the opponent's attack, person A then completes the second half of the transaction by raising and shifting the CL forward and extending, by circling the arms forward, all in a very quick circular movement of receiving and returning.

In the beginning, of necessity, the results were crude, and lack of finesse in execution was frequently compensated for by the use of excessive force. Professor Yu's classes always had a somewhat charged atmosphere due to the large number of large egos attached to the large number of gongfu practitioners. As a result, in its return, force was often compounded with considerable interest and delivered with obvious relish, occasionally leading to loss of cool in heated exchanges.

In the beginning, of necessity, the results were crude, and lack of finesse in execution was frequently compensated for by the use of excessive force.

Nevertheless, learning was accomplished, and as the eighties progressed, I had the opportunity to refine my skills. Under the constant tutelage of Fong Ha in the practice of push-hands, both Taiji and Yiquan style, my crude neutralizing and discharging abilities slowly began to evolve into something approaching the beginnings of an art form.

Yiquan push-hands, often called rolling hands, differs from taichi push-hands in several important ways. First, generally in Taiji, right arm touches right arm and left arm touches left arm of the opponent. In Yiquan it is the opposite: left arm touches right arm and right arm touches left arm. Second, Taiji push-hands uses patterns, whereas

Yiquan uses no set pattern, but seeks to inform all its movement with the awareness of integration. Here all the circular movements of CL and sphere practiced and discovered in shili are used—first to sense the opponent's intentions and neutralize them, and second to discharge jin at the appropriate moment to control the opponent and causing them to lose balance.

The moment of application of force is the moment you detect tension in your opponent, for tension is the gate of access to the opponent's CL. Then the jin is discharged at the point of contact directly into the opponent...

And what is the appropriate moment? The moment of application of force is the moment you detect tension in your opponent, for tension is the gate of access to the opponent's CL. Then the jin is discharged at the point of contact directly into the opponent's CL, causing them to lose balance or bounce away.

6. Master Cai and the Refinement of Jin

As I have recounted in greater detail elsewhere, during the course of the eighties Fong Ha met and began working with Taiji Master Cai Songfang from Canton and Shanghai.[2] Finally in 1987 Fong arranged for Master Cai's first visit to the U.S. We were immediately taken both by his persona and his practice. What was so amazing and appealing to us was the similarity of Master Cai's practice to the Yiquan system, i.e. the inclusion of standing meditation. Here we had tapped into a current in the Taijiquan system similar to what had led to the creation of the Yiquan system out of the Xingyiquan system.

Master Cai exemplifies the principle in the Taijiquan tradition that underneath the proliferation of family styles and their innumerable forms, there also runs a deep current that finds the source of all movement in the

Chapter 9 Using Strength with Awareness

stillness of postural meditation. Master Cai, like the Yiquan system, puts primary emphasis on the development of the Yi (I), or mind intent. Like the Yiquan system, Master Cai's main practice is standing meditation. Like the Yiquan practitioners, Master Cai does not practice forms. In fact, though within the Yang lineage, he does not practice the long form or any set sequences. In the past he practiced the "grasping the bird's tail" sequence and some other movement exercises, but he has since even given those up.

Working with Master Cai over the years of the early nineties helped me to refine and deepen both my practice and physical skills, as well as my conceptual understanding of the uses of stillness and the ideas of integration and fajin.

"... [T]he secret of using yi or intention is that both body and mind should be in a totally relaxed state to begin with, but at the moment of release the posture of the body should become firm, totally unmovable, almost frozen.... By relaxing all the muscles of the body, by relaxing the mind, relaxing both internally and externally, your qi will be able to flow according to your intention. Intention will lead or navigate the qi. The force I feel when I use intention is the qi being directed by my intention.... At the moment of discharge, the qi (energy), the jin (strength) and the yi (intention) all come out at once, but the yi comes out first, because the yi (intention) leads the qi (energy)."[3]

"The secret of using yi or intention is that both body and mind should be in a totally relaxed state to begin with, but at the moment of release the posture of the body should become firm, totally unmovable, almost frozen...."

Understanding the anatomical and physiological mechanisms of discharging energy must begin with a consideration of the polarity structure of the body's musculo-skeletal system. A muscular structure that is

191

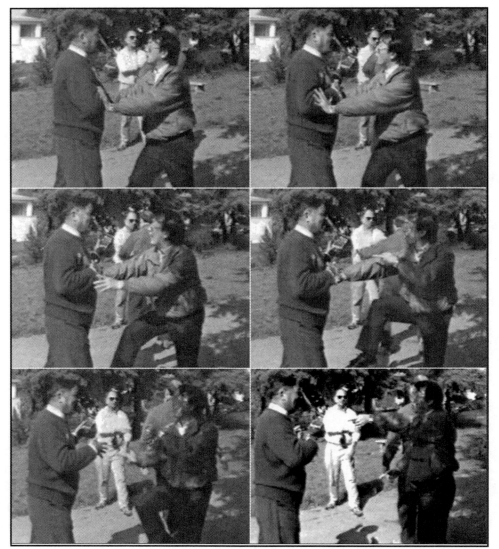

Fig. 9-3. Master Cai demonstrating fajin

paired and opposite creates the dynamic tension of the body, which is what allows for our mobility. If you want to do a certain movement, it requires the contraction of muscle A while its opposite member, muscle B is stretched and lengthened. If you want to move back to the original position, then you must contract muscle B, and muscle A will correspondingly be stretched and lengthened.

Chapter 9 Using Strength with Awareness

Considering that discharge takes place in stillness, and not in movement, the question then becomes: If all movement is produced by the simultaneous contracting-stretching actions of oppositely paired muscles, what muscle action, if any, is involved in the discharge of energy in stillness?

Deane Juhan gives the answer in *Job's Body*: "…[E]ach individual muscle cell has only three options. It can shorten, it can lengthen, or it can lock into place preventing either motion…. From these meager choices, muscle tissue produces all of the postures, gestures and qualities of flesh of which we are capable. We stretch, we contract, and we lock into place; this is, in a nutshell, the entire gamut of our motor behavior."[4]

"We stretch, we contract, and we lock into place; this is, in a nutshell, the entire gamut of our motor behavior."

The "frozen" quality that Master Cai talks about in the stillness is produced by the total simultaneous and instantaneous exertion of all the body's muscular cells locking themselves into place, freezing the body into a posture which literally becomes the embodiment of the mental intention that created it.

However, this freezing must not be thought of as a contraction. It is actually an expansion that originates in our wuji center and proceeds to the periphery where it is constrained by our postural structure and transmitted, or discharged, into whatever we are touching. Biomechanically, this unitary expansion is initiated by "filling the mingmen," i.e. using the pelvic tilt to push out the lumbar spine, thereby integrating the lower and upper parts of the torso.[5]

YIQUAN: THE METHOD OF AWARENESS IN MARTIAL ARTS

In practical terms, in training you must be patient, and in discharging, you must always expand the parts that are opposite the points of contact on your sphere. This means that you must maintain the frame of the arms when being pushed upon, and fill the mingmen only in the lower back. Then the jin will actually discharge from the circle formed by the arms and hands.

What distinguishes the internal martial arts from the external martial arts is the qualitative difference between the initial impulse and the final discharge

This will help you to never think of discharging as expanding forward. This causes a leaning which indicates greediness. Instead, you must only think of expanding backwards, i.e. pushing out at the mingmen. Then the posture itself will conduct the impulse, and you will automatically expand forward in an equal amount and discharge at the periphery of the sphere/hands. For example, when Master Cai is doing pengjin, or expanding energy in postures like "single ward off" and "brush knee forward," he has dual intention—one in the palm pressing down and one in the mingmen—with no intention in the hand/palm at the point of actual contact. The point of contact will accomplish the discharge automatically as the other two intentions expand the sphere while stabilizing its center.

According to Master Cai: In the final analysis, what distinguishes the internal martial arts from the external martial arts is the qualitative difference between the initial impulse and the final discharge. In the internal martial arts the impulse to discharge, like a wave, starts weak in the center of the body and builds so that it is strongest just at the point of contact where it leaves the body. In the external martial arts, on the other hand, the impulse is strongest at the beginning and then its force diminishes as it is discharged at the point of contact on the periphery.

194

Part IV

The Tao (Yin) of Yiquan

Chapter 10

Yiquan and Taijiquan

1. The Polarity of Pengjin

The great Taiji Master Ma Yuehliang ascribed a polarity structure to the concept designated by the word peng. Noting that there are two characters for peng that differ by only one stroke, he distinguished between peng as the neuro-muscular realm (of movement and strength) and peng as the neuro-sensory realm (of stillness and awareness).

Fig. 10-1.
Master Ma Yuehliang

In its yang aspect, Master Ma writes, peng "...means something like structure or framework and people often think this is what is meant by peng."[1] On this neuro-muscular and structural level, peng refers to the functional integration of the body in the ability to absorb and repel an opponent's force. The acquisition of this "yang-peng" is the necessary and sufficient condition enabling the acquisition of jin, or explosive force of internal strength, which was the subject of the previous chapter. It is, however, not the ultimate achievement in the martial arts, for Master Ma exhorts us that, "If you base your Taiji on this incorrect meaning of peng then the whole of your Taiji will be incorrect."[2]

The greater accomplishment is the acquisition of the skill associated with "yin-peng," which pertains to the realm of the neuro-sensory and internal awareness. In

197

fact, Master Ma prescribes the total subordination of yang-peng and its neuro-muscular strength to the yin-peng of neuro-sensory awareness. The yin "pengjin is over the whole body and it is used to measure the strength and direction of the partner's force…. It should be so light that the weight of a feather will make it move. It can be described like water which will, with no intention of its own, support equally the weight of a floating leaf or the weight of a floating ship." Thus, "pengjin is sensitivity."[3]

"Pengjin is over the whole body and it is used to measure the strength and direction of the partner's force…. pengjin is sensitivity."

This yin notion of pengjin then is the subject of the fourth and last part of this book. It will serve us as a vehicle to greater understanding, not only of the relationship between Yiquan and Taijiquan, but also, ultimately, of martial art as a path of developmental transformation and spiritual growth.

2. Wang Xiangzhai and Taijiquan

The genius of Wang Xiangzhai was his ability to synthesize. He was able to assimilate the essence of many other schools into a system of essences. Thus, the uniqueness of the Yiquan lies in the fact that it is a meta-system of health and martial arts. For example, for health, he incorporated into his standing practice "the quintessence of Qigong breathing and stretching skills from Confucian, Buddhist and Taoist schools."[4] He believed and taught that ultimate achievement in martial arts required that yang and yin faculties and functions of the body-mind, as embodied in different martial arts, be uniquely honed so that they supplement and complement one another.

The yin-yang referred to here is the same basic polarity

Chapter 10   Yiquan and Taijiquan

of peng introduced by Master Ma. Anatomically and biologically, the peng polarity is built into our nervous system, a function of the afferent and efferent nerves that deal, respectively, with incoming and outgoing messages. The efferent nervous system produces yin peng because it is receptive and passive—the realm of awareness and attention. The afferent system produces yang peng because it is executive in nature—it decides and acts, it is the realm of will and intention.

Fig. 10-2.
Wang   Xiangzhai

To find the ultimate balance and reach the true pinnacle of the Art of Quan, Grandmaster Wang combined the yin-yang of the internal martial arts. Traditionally, the Xingyi system as a whole is considered the yang pole, as it is the more power oriented system, whereas the Taiji system is considered the yin pole or more awareness oriented system. Grandmaster Wang chose "xingyiquan's mechanisms of force characterized by completeness and solidness as the basis..."[5] of his martial art. The very name "Yiquan" expresses its efferent orientation of control and will, of musculo-skeletal force directed by mental will and intent.

Fig 10-3.
Yang   Chengfu

Wang Xiangzhai turned to Taijiquan to incorporate its essence of cultivating the yin, the efferent nervous system, and its emphasis on the martial uses of yielding and mindfulness. In the words of Wang Xuanjie, "...[H]e incorporated into his new boxing Taijiquan's four skills of attaching, sticking, joining and following, as well as its soft way of exerting force...."[6] Wang Xiangzhai himself wrote, "Among disciples by direct line of Taijiquan, I think the most outstanding masterhands are the Yang brothers, Yang Shaohou and Yang Chengfu."[7] He considered himself "as an intimate friend of theirs" and valued their "genuine knowledge of mechanics in Taijiquan." [8]

Indeed, grandmaster Yang Chengfu's mastery of the unity of perceptive and proprioceptive awareness was legendary. One of the most telling stories relating this was his ability to hold a bird in his open palm without the bird being able to fly away. In order to fly away, the bird has to flex its legs to push off. When it did so Yang Chengfu would relax and yield to the bird's pushing off with the legs, literally causing the ground underneath the bird's feet to vanish, thereby disabling the ability to take flight.

Each generation of Yiquan practitioners must retrace the steps of Wang Xiangzhai and balance the inherent yangness of the Yiquan system with the yin emphasis of the Taiji system.

Wang Xiangzhai himself was famous for the application of this exquisite ability in controlling his opponents in the game of push-hands. He always told his students that "when you push people...they should have an easy sensation of comfort and make them feel as if they've never been pushed before like that in their life and then they will ask you, 'Will you please push me again?'" [9]

It seems as if each generation of Yiquan practitioners must retrace the steps of Wang Xiangzhai and balance the inherent yangness of the Yiquan system with the yin neuro-sensory emphasis of the Taiji system. Failing that, the Yiquan yang peng will predominate ,and yin peng will not be achieved. Unfortunately, this yin aspect is also the hardest to transmit, and as a result, most Yiquan practitioners in the world today have not developed it and continue to operate strictly on the level of force.

For example, Guo Lianying, the famous Taiji and Shaolin Master who taught for years in San Francisco, was one of Wang Xiangzhai's early students. Including Xingyiquan and Yiquan in the larger historical substrate from which they originated, Kuo wrote:

Fig 10-4.
Master Guo Lianying

"First to have then not to have. This is why it is best to first enter the gates of Shaolin. Then you already have Shaolin's strength. Your base is stable and the body's vitality is brimming with energy. Afterward, enter the gate of Taiji. From the beginning Chang Sanfen, Yang Luchan, Chang Songxi, Jie Fengzhi, and other great masters came this way. They all had refined their peerless Shaolin as a foundation and then shifted to Taiji. They ascended the boundary of spiritual change".[10]

3. Yu Pengxi and Empty Force

The history and teachings of Professor Yu Pengxi, who was one of Wang Zhiang Zhai's top students, also clearly mirrors the founder's process of turning to Taijiquan. In the previous chapter I recounted the yang, neuro-muscular, side of the professor's training methods in the practice of discharging integral force. Here I want to detail the yin, neuro-sensory, side of the professor's training methods as expressed in his practice of "kongjin," or "empty force," the apparent art of moving someone at a distance,

Fig 10-5.
Master Yu Pengxi

Fig 10-6. Prof Yu using 'empty force'

without touching them.

The development of empty force seems to have been mainly a Shanghainese phenomenon. Though from different systems, both of my teachers who practiced empty force, Professor Yu (Yiquan) and Cai Songfang (Taijiquan), were from Shanghai, and could trace their use of empty force back to a Taiji Master named Le Huangzhi. As a top student of Dong Yinjie, considered by many Yang Chengfu's best student, Le Huangzhi was a big name in the pre-World War II world of Shanghai Taiji.

Professor Yu's connection with Le Huangzhi was direct. He invited Le Huangzhi to come and stay at his house to teach him about empty force and teach his wife the Taiji form. Master Cai's ties to Le Huangzhi are more indirect, almost environmental. Master Cai said he never personally witnessed Le Huangzhi, but heard about his "empty force" ability through Le Huangzhi's son. Author of one of the classic books on Taijiquan entitled *The Essential Principle*, Le Huangzhi's son was Master Cai's college friend and fellow martial arts enthusiast. Also one of Master Cai's own teachers, Master Guo Dadong, had been a student of Master Le Huangzhi in the mid-fifties and had personally experienced his "empty force."

Chapter 10   Yiquan and Taijiquan

The term kongjin, or empty force, is used because the Master seems to be controlling his opponent from a distance, moving him at will. Today there are few practices in the Chinese martial arts that generate more dispute and controversy than the use of empty force. Some swear to its irresistibility while others sneer at it as empty "farce." Both of these extreme assessments are based on misunderstanding the simple truth that, basically, what we have is a game of perception, not force.

Even in Le Huangzhi's time, great misunderstandings and misrepresentations regarding the nature and use of empty force created ongoing controversy within the world of internal martial arts. Zheng Manqing, for example, did not think much of Le Huangzhi and his talent: "I knew Li. His Taiji was not too good. He could do the thing you mention (empty force) but only because you are a student. The trick will not work against an equal or a superior."[11]

> Zheng Manqing did not think much of Le Huangzhi and his talent: "I knew Li. His Taiji was not too good. He could do the thing you mention (empty force) but only because you are a student. The trick will not work against an equal or a superior."

4. The Genesis of Empty Force

The Taijiquan system and tradition, particularly Yang family style, is famous for its theoretical and practical emphasis on the neuro-sensory over the neuro-muscular. The traditional precept is that "awareness overcomes strength and technique." The development of Kongjin or empty force awareness is a logical outgrowth of this orientation of the Taijiquan tradition. Empty force is the most refined extension of tingjin, the ability to listen to and interpret energy, which we try to cultivate in push-hands practice.

THE TAO OF YIQUAN

When we begin push-hands practice our touch is inevitably very heavy because we are still coming from the point of view of strength. But as we progress we begin to experience that relaxation and softness overcomes strength and hardness; push-hands becomes touch-hands. As our touch naturally becomes lighter and lighter, we begin to understand how awareness overcomes technique. Taken to its extreme in kongjin (empty force), we no longer touch at all because the interplay occurs on the energetic level between the two fields of awareness.

As we progress we begin to experience that relaxation and softness overcomes strength and hardness ...and understand how awareness overcomes technique.

Master Cai discovered how it worked for himself one day in 1974 in Guangdong. He was working with an exceptionally perceptive and sensitive student. It was almost by accident, Master Cai said, that at one point he used only his intention, exerting no physical force, and yet his student moved away! When he realized the implications of his discovery, he started a process of further experimentation. With some of his students and friends, he began a program of systematic practice in the training of awareness and intention.

The genesis of empty force is in the closely interpenetrating fields of a near-contact situation. From personal experience in pushing hands with masters Yu and Cai I became extremely sensitized to the sphere of their physical influence, the space within their reach. Here I discovered non-contact to be more dangerous than contact, in that even when not touching, the field of our interacting awarenesses was very charged and powerful. I knew that, perceptually speaking, they had already disarmed me with their awareness, taking control of my center. In this relationship: when they intend, I jump. Thus, true empty force is the merger of and control over one field of awareness by another without physical contact but within physical reach.

5. Empty Force as a Game of Awareness

However, a different situation exists when the interaction is outside of the physical reach of the players. Then the interaction takes on the character of a game that is played according to certain rules. In this game, there is a sender and a receiver. The rule of the game is an agreement, conscious or unconscious, between the sender and the receiver. Like a marionette on invisible strings, the receiver embodies, or acts out in movement, the perceived intent of the sender.

True empty force is the merger of and control over one field of awareness by another without physical contact but within physical reach.

If the receiver perceives being pushed back, they go back; if they perceive being pulled forward, they go forward; if they perceive being shoved to the left or right, they move accordingly. If they perceive a somersault intention, they will somersault; if they perceive a pirouette, they will pirouette. If they perceive a strong intention, they will react strongly; if they perceive a weak one, they will react in mild movement. As familiarity increases, the range of play naturally extends out—infinitely, at least in theory, stretching the perceptual limits of their fields into more subtle interchange. Playing this game, I would jump 20 to 30 feet by only a look from Masters Yu or Cai.

The person moves only because they have agreed to do so under the rules of the game. What is really developed in this training is that very special type of awareness and sensitivity, the so-called sixth sense, of field awareness that embraces but also goes beyond its visual or auditory components. This is dramatically illustrated in the kind of awareness that many blind people develop in compensation for the loss of sight. When you are in a room full of people that includes a blind person and you look at that blind person with a strong stare or intention, more likely than not that person will feel that somebody is looking at him/her and turn around or otherwise respond. Like many blind people, animals or so-called "primitive" peoples have retained this sixth sense of presence or awareness of intention.

In the evolutionary scheme of things, the distance senses of vision and hearing developed after the proximity senses of touch and taste. In fact, vision can be thought of as an extension of the sense of touch, a form of touching at a distance. Its survival value, obviously, consists of giving us quicker information regarding possible threats to our being before the threat is literally upon us, giving us more time to prepare and activate our defense systems. The true benefit of kongjin play is the development of distance field awareness; obviously this ability has great usefulness in the martial arts. Anybody can look across the room with a strong intention. But the ability to feel that intention as an intrusion into the field of awareness is possessed by very few indeed.

Fig. 10-7. Prof. Yu using empty force on two people

6. The Limitations of Empty Force

The greatest limitation in the idea and practice of distance empty force comes from the confusion it engenders in the minds of the observing public, and sometimes participants alike, who equate "empty force" with "irresistible force." When John Q Public observes the kongjin game in action, they are liable to draw the wrong conclusion by focusing on the sender rather than the receiver. They're liable to say, "Gee this guy is so powerful he can move people and make them do things from a distance." But in fact, it is the receiving/perceiving skill that is being cultivated and practiced.

The second and deeper level of confusion occurs when the receivers themselves actually begin to believe that they are being moved against their will from a distance; the illusion becomes a delusion. Ironically, renouncing their critical faculties in favor of this belief actually creates the reality of the practitioners' vulnerability.

The third and deepest level of confusion is when the sender begins to believe that they are moving people at a distance against their will, resulting in behavioral delusions of grandeur.

I had different experiences in my practice of kongjin with Master Cai and Professor Yu. With Master Cai, there was never any doubt as to what was being practiced. Master Ha recalled his first experience with Master Cai's empty force while visiting him in Canton, China in 1979. "When I saw him working with his students, they would jump back 20-30 feet when he merely pointed at them. At first I could hardly believe my eyes, figuring it had to be either a miracle or a joke. But in discussing it with him, he explained to me that they were merely playing with the intention and its perception—in other words, with subtle energy, not irresistible force. Then when I played push-hands with his students, I quickly understood its value. They were so sensitive and quick that at that time I could not push them. They perceived and were able to neutralize my intention to push them the very moment I had it. That was a real eye opener."

With Professor Yu and his students the situation was more ambiguous. Undoubtedly, the language barrier was a big factor in the obfuscation of the practice that took place. But there can be little doubt that there were many, many of his students who convinced themselves they were being moved by irresistible forces at a distance. I do not know what Professor Yu believed himself on the subject, but there is also no doubt that he did nothing to demystify the practice and discourage such limiting beliefs and perceptions on the part of his students. On the contrary, it was always a good show. Personally, after a few years of increasingly reluctant participation, I discontinued my studies with him.

There can be little doubt that there were many, many of Prof. Yu's students who convinced themselves they were being moved by irresistible forces at a distance.

Yet, evaluating my training with Professor Yu now, some 15 years later, I see both its value and limitations. The training emphasized the practice of the extreme yin and yang poles of the awareness-integral strength continuum. His "empty force" was extreme yin and the "bong-bong" exercises, described in the last chapter, represented the extreme yang. His teaching strategy evidently was that practicing the extremes of the yin-yang

Chapter 10   Yiquan and Taijiquan

polarity would eventually cause strength and awareness to interpenetrate and balance each other.

In my own case, I did not achieve the integration of strength and awareness by means of his training practice and methods. Perhaps I was not ready for it, but I also believe it is more than that. Prof. Yu's system, for all intents and purposes, was a no-touch system. In ban-ban practice the emphasis on strength effectively eliminates touch as a training parameter, and of course in his empty force there is no touch involved at all. By cultivating only the extremes of the spectrum, his system lacked the integrating factor of the sense of touch and the development of tactile yin peng.

Prof. Yu's teaching strategy evidently was that practicing the extremes of the yin-yang polarity would eventually cause strength and awareness to interpenetrate and balance each other.

This insight was born, admittedly, out of hindsight after working for the past four years with Master Sam Tam from Vancouver. As the next two chapters will detail, Master Tam's incredible art is that his consciousness surfs the interface of attention and intention at the point(s) of contact with the opponent with such delicacy and precision that he is able to control him with no force at all, only awareness.

Chapter 11

Stillness and Movement with Master Tam

1. Meeting Sam Tam

I first met Sam Tam in the mid-seventies when he began to come down from Vancouver periodically to visit with Fong Ha. His letter of introduction had been instrumental in introducing Fong Ha to Master Han, and his first visits coincided with the stays of Master Han.

At that time, Sam already had a reputation as a highly skilled fighter and practitioner of the Eagle Claw and Yiquan systems. Though not himself a teacher of these arts, on his visits he would often demonstrate them, astonishing us with his skills of fajin discharging and joint locking. Age-wise only a few years my senior, in terms of skill and ability he was then, and has remained through the years, light-years ahead of me.

Fig. 11-1 Master Sam Tam

In the years of the early and mid nineties, Sam's own transformational process led him to withdraw from much outside contact and our Bay Area group did not see much of him. As it turns out, his process of discovery was very similar to those of his Yiquan predecessors Wang Xiangzhai and Yu Pengxi's, and entailed turning to Taijiquan for the balancing yin complement to Yiquan's yang.

When he reappeared and began to share the fruits of his transformation with us, enormous vistas of developmental possibility opened up that I had previously read about but never experienced. This involved the method of using no force, only awareness, to control your opponent in push-hands practice.

As of this writing Sam has been coming down several times a year to conduct workshops with us in the Bay Area, and I've also been fortunate enough to be invited up to Vancouver periodically for further instruction. During all of these sessions, quite a bit of videotaping was done, with the result that a record exists of many of his patient attempts to get across to us slow-witted students the basic concepts of his method. What I have tried to do in this and the following chapter is to weave together many of his spontaneous comments, instructions, and insights contained in these videos into a more or less logical sequence, taking such editorial liberties as required to render speech into written narrative.

2. Sam Tam and Taijiquan

I found out that flaunting your strength and using force doesn't make you any friends. Of course that's not right, because we are here on this planet in order to get along.

"As you remember, I used to come down to the Bay Area from Vancouver 10-15 years ago to exchange ideas with and contest my peers, many of whom are now respected Bay Area teachers. Generally I was respected and feared, but not that well liked. And although I never hurt anyone, people feared my skills of Yiquan fajin discharge and Eagle Claw locking methods.

"But I found out that flaunting your strength and using force doesn't make you any friends. Of course that's not right, because we are here on this planet in order to get along. So that made me think a lot about the limitations of the use of force as a method of exercising control of one's situation.

"Then a chance meeting in a Vancouver Park brought me into direct contact with that wonderful Chinese tradition based in the knowledge that being big and strong is not necessarily a guarantee of success in physical conflict. Speed, timing, and awareness are other skills that give the smaller and weaker the possibility of victory.

"While practicing my Yiquan zhanzhuang I was approached by a frail, not so healthy-looking elderly gentleman who told me, 'You're using too much force; you have to give up your force in order to develop more feeling and awareness. Then you will be able to control people with no force, with only your awareness. Let me show you.'

The old gentleman was a Yang family style Taiji Master, who practiced the secret southern fighting form of 37 movements that originated with Yang Pan Hou, and which was popularized in the U.S. by the late Zheng Manqing.

"It turns out the old gentleman was a Yang family style Taiji Master, who practiced the secret southern fighting form of 37 movements that originated with Yang Panhou, and which was popularized in the U.S. by the late Zheng Manqing. When he shared with me his ability to control the opponent with no force, I was very impressed. I then began to reread all the classics and practice differently, and eventually I also had the breakthrough to where I was able to give up the use of force and use no-force to control a situation simply with my awareness.

"And actually life has become a lot more fun since then, for when no-force is used in controlling a situation, it is a pleasant experience for both the controller and the controlled. For it is a curious fact that when you are controlled by no-force, you don't mind it, and in fact find

Fig. 11-2. "Finding the Light in the Heavy" -1

it enjoyable. This aspect of fun and good feeling generated by the practice has made me eager to share this method of awareness with more people.

"You must remember that standing, Taiji, Yiquan, Yijin-jing, all these things are but tools to lead you to the ultimate goal: the development of awareness both as method and goal. Since they are but the means, do not invest them with the importance of the ends. Its like the old saying: When you go fishing, the bait is important, for you will put it on the line to catch the fish; but once you've caught the fish the bait is no longer important.

Fig. 11-3. "Finding the Light in the Heavy" -2

"Now in the old times when you were learning, you would often see the teacher stand still before beginning the Taiji form. As a student, you weren't really told what he was doing, but eventually you began to understand that actually he was checking his postural alignments before moving. The deeper lesson of this practice is that you move only when alignment of mind

214

and body has been accomplished and you are aware of it. In other words, you must move only with mindfulness.

"We have to begin at the beginning. If you're going to be in a physical encounter, first of all you have to be able to stand up straight by yourself, for if you can't do that, you will be unable to stand straight under attack by an opponent. So the way I'm showing you is to maintain your posture in what is called the pile stance. As we will see, every requirement we impose is an awareness we try to develop; therefore, in this pile standing stance, everything has a purpose."

3. The Spine and Central Equilibrium

"Central in our practice, then, is awareness of postural alignment. You must have a straight back (spine) first, because spinal alignment produces awareness of our central equilibrium. To straighten the spine, we work at both ends of it, first the top and then the bottom.

"Begin by thinking about your head as hanging from the sky by a string. The point where you imagine the string to be attached is not the top of the skull. Rather, it is attached at "the secret point" deep in the brain, created by the intersection of (1) the line between the ears and (2) the line from the point between the eyes to the back of the head.

"To draw this line correctly, and to create a straight spine, you must lightly pull back the ears and tuck the chin. If the chin is not in, the head and spine (body) are not integrated and it will be easy for your opponent to push

The way I'm showing you is to maintain your posture in what is called the pile stance. As we will see, every requirement we impose is an awareness we try to develop; therefore, in this pile standing stance, everything has a purpose.

Fig. 11-4. Master Tam demonstrating #1 standing posture

you back. Therefore, the chin tucked in and the shoulders rounded, as we'll talk about in a minute, are necessary for the centerline to be integrated -making you strong so that you cannot be pushed around easily.

"Now let's examine the lower part of the spine and its integration with the upper part. If you think about the upper part of the body and spine as being pulled up, then to straighten the spine, you must think of the lower part of the body and spine as sinking, as being pulled down by gravity. This is often referred to as sinking the energy or qi into the dantien, or lower abdominal area.

If you think about the upper part of the body and spine as being pulled up, then to straighten the spine, you must think of the lower part of the body and spine as sinking, as being pulled down by gravity.

"This sinking feeling is facilitated by the use of the pelvic tilt. So you must pull your tail bone and pelvic floor forward and upward. This action gets rid of the lumbar curve in the spine, straightening it and thereby effectively integrating upper and lower torso.

"You need only be aware of two points—not one, not many—of the centerline. If you have only the point of the center, you will be easily uprooted. If you're trying to align three points or more, it's too many and therefore too slow. Allow your awareness to rest on the top and bottom points."

4. Structure of the Sphere

The shoulders must be made round, as if spreading your wings. Push them out sideways and then curve them forward. A slight hollowing of the chest should result and be experienced.

"The shoulders must be made round, as if spreading your wings. Push them out sideways and then curve them forward. A slight hollowing of the chest should result and be experienced.

"Rounding the shoulders integrates the whole body. When you do it right, your whole structure is solid, and you will be able to absorb any hit more efficiently and easily. Even the rib cage can stand a lot of pressure when the shoulders are rounded. Thus, round shoulders will act

Fig. 11-5.   Master Tam in Universal Pose

Fig. 11-6. Standing Practice with Master Tam

as a force shield and prevent punches from penetrating. Conversely, not rounding the shoulders is asking for trouble. It's like saying: Please hit me, I'm at my most vulnerable.

The roundness of the shoulders integrates with the straightness of the spine for the naturally efficient utilization of the rotational aspect of the centerline.

"Being round-shouldered is also essential in helping you be able to move quickly and appropriately. The roundness of the shoulders integrates with the straightness of the spine for the naturally efficient utilization of the rotational aspect of the centerline. Simply put, people will be unable to push on you because when they try, whether they push fast or slow, a little or a lot, your response will always be appropriate, diverting their force to one side or the other by the proper turning of the body.

"When you round the shoulders properly, automatically the elbows will move forward and away from the body at diagonal angles. Then, keeping your elbows steady, turn your forearms and, with palms facing up, raise them upward in front of and aligned with their respective shoulders. The image is as if you're holding or embracing a big fragile ball. If you hold it too hard, the ball will break,

218

and if you hold it too lightly, it will blow away. Therefore have relaxed awareness of what is sufficient strength.

"I prefer the "hold the ball" posture as the primary meditation posture because it helps to integrate the arms with the torso, while opening up the upper lungs. Do you feel the difference while breathing? This way, the upper lungs can take in more air. But if you want to hold the wuji posture with the arms hanging down by the sides, you should at least turn the palms of the hands to the back and have the elbows slightly away from the body. This will help prevent the shoulders from getting stuck and inhibit the free expansion and contraction of the upper chest in breathing.

I prefer the "hold the ball" posture as the primary meditation posture because it helps to integrate the arms with the torso, while opening up the upper lungs.

5. The Foundation of the Legs

"The legs are the foundation we stand on, and their integration with the torso in postures allows the three movements of the centerline.

"The hips allow the rotational movement of the torso around the centerline. To facilitate awareness of this, after you have straightened the spine, give yourself the mental suggestion to relax and sink into the hips—literally, maybe an inch or so.

"The knees allow the vertical movement of the centerline. To maintain a sense of readiness for action, the knees are unlocked and from slightly to half-way bent, ready to extend to move the torso. Feel as if there is an expanding balloon between them that you are slightly squeezing with the knees to counter its imaginary expansion.

"The ankles allow horizontal shifting movement. There are two basic stances: the parallel stance is mostly for cultivation, and the archer stance with one foot forward is mostly for movement. The actual size of stance is different for everyone, with the measurement being, for both parallel and archer stance, the outside width of the shoulders.

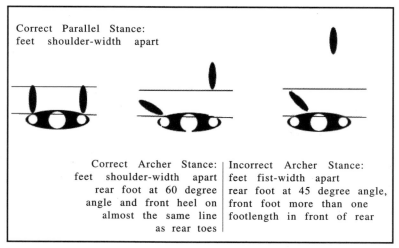

Fig. 11-9. Position of the feet

Chapter 11   Stillness and Movement with Master Tam

"The shoulder-width archer stance makes for a wider channel, while the basic angle between front and rear foot is about 60 degrees. This is slightly different from what many of you are used to: a longer stance with a narrower channel (the width of a fist), and the rear foot angled out 45 degrees. Traditionally, these narrow stances were used only with weapons, in order to avoid lopping off one's own appendages. It will take a little to get used to this different alignment. But just remember that however you stand, if you move the front foot back, the feet should be shoulder width apart. That's the principle."

6. Circular Movement

"Standing is a kind of measurement of what you are ready to achieve; if you cannot do what you want to when you stand still, how can you think about doing it while moving? You must first integrate your body in standing before you move with it as an integrated unit. Then when you do move, you must always use a circular motion; never a straight force; it is the circle that contains the secret of using no force.

You must first integrate your body in standing before you move with it as an integrated unit. Then when you do move, you must always use a circular motion...it is the circle that contains the secret of using no force.

"The two primary circular movements are the horizontal and the vertical. The horizontal circle is accomplished through the rotation of the centerline. The vertical circle is accomplished through a combination of vertical and horizontal movements of the centerline. In the archer stance the vertical circle is made by a combination of, first, backward shifting and downward sinking, and then forward shifting and upward rising. Naturally they can be combined to make an infinite numbers of diagonal circles.

The size of the circles you make depends on your purpose. For teaching and learning you must make big movements. When I'm teaching, I'm making circles with very big movements for the sake of clarity, to show the path, so there can be no mistake. Practicing with your fellow students, you should also make big circles, so you can figure out where and with whom the movement is going wrong.

For teaching and learning you must make big movements ...when the situation calls for the real use of circles for self-defense, the movement should be done solely with awareness and only very small internal circles.

Over time in practice you make the circles smaller and smaller until all movement is internalized. Thus when the situation calls for the real use of circles for self-defense, the movement should be done solely with awareness and only very small internal circles. To see no visible external movement and not knowing that I am coming, that's the most terrible and dangerous part of it for my opponent."

Chapter 12

Master Tam and the Practice of No-Force

1. Using Force

"Basically, there are two different ways of establishing control in a situation. You either attempt to control through strength or through awareness. When using strength, I distinguish three different ways. On the most elementary level of using strength, without regard for control of balance, people will lean with their body weight into their opponent when pushed. The shortcomings of this approach need hardly be discussed.

"A slightly higher level is that used in most martial arts. Here usually the arms and hands act as if separated from the rest of the body, resulting in a fragmented and partial strength. This is why in meditation we emphasize using the hands as if holding a ball so that the arms become part of the body and its total strength of exertion.

Fig. 12-1. Master Tam making a point.

"When the torso, arms and legs are integrated, you have what is called the frame. In martial arts use, this frame is very important. First, it is indispensable for developing the ability to take your opponent's force into the ground. Second, the frame is the vehicle for the discharge of jin, or concentrated energy, at the point of contact. Without development of the frame and the ability to use it, higher levels of martial arts are impossible.

"In Chinese the frame is referred to as your peng. Once you experience it, you understand why it is described as a <u>sphere</u> of force and awareness. Because no matter where you touch me, my peng is right there and I can focus and discharge my jin from any point of the sphere, i.e., from any part of my body. The jin is like the shock wave from the center to the periphery of the sphere, where it is discharged into the opponent at the point of contact.

I tell you that fajin is elementary, because it still operates on the muscular level and is played out in terms of strength and force. There is yet a higher level of control that we can reach by developing the deeper skills of perceptual awareness.

"Martial artists who have developed an integrated frame, rooting, and fajin achieve the most sophisticated level of using force. In this case the force is both delivered and received in an upright posture with control of the centerline and equilibrium. In this method, when my opponent touches me I absorb the force and root myself into the floor with it through the pile structure developed by standing meditation. Then I can issue it back into my opponent as fajin at the point of contact.

"Having the frame, being integrated, knowing how to root and issue (fajin) are very often thought of as the highest possible development in the martial arts. But I tell you that fajin is elementary, because it still operates on the muscular level and is played out in terms of strength and force. There is yet a higher level of control that we can reach by developing the deeper skills of perceptual awareness."

2. Using No Force

"This is a developmental process that moves gradually from using great force to using no force, only awareness. First it is necessary to develop the strength, integration, centerline, and rooting that we've talked about—only then can we give it up, properly and with results. It's just like money: If you want to be a philanthropist and give away a lot of money, you must first have accumulated it somehow; otherwise there's nothing to get rid of.

"Responding with no force at the point of contact at the moment of touch is the key to control. When you experience force from your opponent, you must let go and yield, while maintaining contact, and not respond with your strength against his strength. Never fight your opponent's force. If you encounter force, you must yield first and then push. Move forward and backward, sink and rise, turn right and left, as required, but resist the temptation to fight with me when I use force. Yield to it to uproot me and then give it back with complete effortlessness. That's the circle.

"When you touch someone, you know they are doing the right thing when you meet no force yet feel as if you and your energy are being sucked into them. Here, you try: When you touch me, there's nothing there, there is nothing to land on and you feel as if you're caught. I don't lose touch with you, my hand is always there, aimed at your center, and my body is loose, ready to uproot you at any moment.

This method of control through no force is far more disconcerting to the opponent than the use of force.

"This method of control through no-force is far more disconcerting to the opponent than the use of force. For example, when you try to touch me, I am simply not there, like a phantom disappearing as you appear. Thus, you will have no information about my centerline, but I can sense your tension and through it control your centerline.

Fig. 12-2. Push-hands Workshop

Uprooting and moving the opponent with no-force requires that either nothing moves or everything moves
together as a unit and in a circular pattern, with your peng
so sensitive that it floats like a feather on the river of your
opponent's strength.

"In push-hands, along with the use of force, you must
also give up the frame, rooting, and the centerline. By that
I mean that you must stop making them accessible to your
opponents by letting them feel your frame and center
through the point of contact. Doing this makes the point
of contact the point of application, and people will be able
to fajin you. So giving up the frame and centerline, making
it inaccessible to your opponent, means you are taking
away their ability to discharge on you. This is one great
advantage of using not strength but awareness to control
your opponent.

In push-hands, along with the use of force, you must also give up the frame, rooting and the centerline.

226

Chapter 12 Master Tam and the Practice of No-Force

"When challenged, the basic principle is to keep the centerline straight and maintain central equilibrium. Everything, all force detected and received, must be taken in to the centerline and the spine. At the same time, always make your centerline as small as possible; leave no room for your opponent to find it. How do you refine it? By using force neither in receiving nor issuing. For if you push me and I resist, then you will know where my centerline is, and I will have to use force to uproot you. But when you try to push me, and I respond by yielding only, there is no force, and yet you will be uprooted. Thus, if my centerline is small and you can't find it, then I can use no-force to uproot you.

...always make your centerline as small as possible, leave no room for your opponent to find it.

"In ordinary push-hands, when people use force, the outcome is never quite clear and clean. Control is achieved by moving the opponent in a struggling way, so there's always some dispute. But when you are moved by no-force, it is always clean and there is never any dispute.

"Another advantage is that by not using strength, your energy will not be exhausted as soon, and you will last a lot longer. This becomes more important of course the

Fig. 12-3. Giving Corrections (1)

older we get. Finally, it's just a lot more fun and less dangerous, both for controller and controlled, to use awareness rather than force.

"Most students use a lot of strength unconsciously. For example, they all have a tendency to lean with their centerline and use their weight on other people. This should not be done; it must be given up. Any time that you use force, it is too much. It does not get you where you want to go, to the level of awareness and no-force. Also, you must not be so eager to push, and if you are, you must conceal that intention, because if you put it out like that, you're using force and you give opportunity to your opponent.

"Many teachers even, while emphasizing the centerline, still use strength. When you touch them, they feel like a sack of rice—partly soft and partly hard—and when they push, you can feel it coming. When opponents use strength, you can still best them, even though they are stronger. If they allow you to feel their centerline, then they will have to noodle and squirm to get out of it. But if they're good, you can't feel their center. Then what can you push? Where are they? You're touching them but you're losing balance. This is the higher level.

"Once you fight with your strength in push-hands, you're finished. First of all, if anyone comes along who's bigger than you, you're finished. And secondly, if anyone smaller who knows how to use no-force comes along, you're finished too.

With most people, the point of contact is the point of application of force. That is their great weakness. Give the point of contact, but don't allow the point of contact to become the point of application of force."

With most people, the point of contact is the point of application of force. That is their great weakness. Give the point of contact, but don't give you the point of application of force.

3. Using Attention

"The aim is to control the opponent with minimum strength and maximum awareness. The method or strategy is to confound your opponent's nervous system. This begins before the actual moment of touch. Before ever touching, you take stock by observing the body as a whole, judging its level of integration, and cracks in the integration, for access to the centerline. Also, you want to observe the eyes and judge their level of alertness and confidence.

"At the point of contact and the moment of touch, you physically confound the nervous system of your opponent. This is at the core of the ability to uproot and send your opponent flying with no force. I repeat, you must be able to uproot them first, because once they are uprooted, there will be no dispute. And when you are using no-force, even as you are uprooting your opponents, they don't feel it, and when they do feel it, they are not threatened by it.

Control begins with uprooting. You want your opponent's feet ... because when their feet start to wobble, they are uprooted and once uprooted, there is no dispute.

"Control begins with uprooting. You want your opponent's feet to move first, not the body or the hand, because when their feet start to wobble, they are uprooted and once uprooted, there is no dispute. So at the moment of touch, when you cause them to fall into emptiness by just putting your intention somewhere beyond the point of contact, you uproot them, and they will go.

"In your touch and contact, be like a waving flag: your opponent can touch you, but cannot push you, for you disappear and yield wherever they push. In pushing, once your opponent touches you, you make a circle with them and use the force that they supplied and return it to them. In fighting it's the same, but different; you still turn to yield, but in the return circle, you will hit or do whatever you want".

4. Using Intention

"This is the point at which you show what kind of martial artist and human being you are. For once uprooted, your opponent is at your mercy and you decide

Chapter 12   Master Tam and the Practice of No-Force

what to do with them: either use force to inflict physical punishment or use no force at all, but simply control them to prevent their harming you.

"It is clear to me that of the two options, the second is the more mature and spiritually sound path. It allows any attack, whether simulated or real, to become an opportunity to practice compassion. To me, it is this ability to control your opponent with no-force and with kindness that is worth pursuing and developing. Because in this type of training, hard feelings between players don't develop; everyone involved winds up having fun and feeling good.

"Pursuing this path, then, we understand the basic fact is that once someone is uprooted, it really takes very minimal physical force to intensify their loss of balance and control where they go. What is needed and what we want is to develop a keen sense of timing, an exquisite sense of touch, and a strong intention. So after uprooting, we don't use force or even think of pushing our opponent physically. Instead we use the mind to project our intention through the backbone (spine) to some distance in back of them—like picking a target and focusing on it.

What is needed and what we want is to develop a keen sense of timing, an exquisite sense of touch, and a strong intention.

"It is very much like playing ball. When you hit a golf ball, or a ping pong ball, or shoot a basketball, the awareness and intention is not on the point of contact with the ball, but on where the ball is going; and you just do it, with the mind out there. The common mistake in our practice is for your intention to stop at the beginning of the opponent's body, rather than projecting it through them.

231

Fig. 12-4. Giving Corrections (2)

"Once you have your opponent uprooted, extend your intention. If you push me up, I simply turn it against you. And if somebody is pushing down on you, you can use that against him by yielding and circling overhead to hit them. Because of their downward momentum, they will be uprooted and unable to deal with your discharge.

...you must have the body to deliver what is intended by the mind. ... That's why we do standing meditation: to prepare the mind to lead and the body to obey.

"In the relationship of body and mind, we know that thinking is one thing and doing is another. In this case, the thinking is more important than the physical doing, because, as the old saying goes, "the yi (intention) leads the qi (energy/force)." Of course, you must have the body to deliver what is intended by the mind. But the body is not the decision maker; that is the mind. That's why we do standing meditation: to prepare the mind to lead and the body to obey."

5. Sticking

"When you can touch and feel me, but you cannot push me, that is called sticking. Sticking is a kind of offensive listening skill. That means I just follow your force wherever it goes and continue to zero in on your centerline with no force, but awareness. When I stick to you this way, it's the evenness that throws you off balance when you can find nothing to push. I give you the point of contact, but I don't give you the point of application of force against me—while I know the point of application of force against you. I can feel you coming, but you can't feel me coming. Therefore I don't resist you, but go wherever you want to go, and I use no-force to uproot and control you.

"Sticking is the most terrible predicament, in a way. When you find you are pushing someone and you cannot get away because you will loose your balance if you try to disengage, giving them the opportunity to hit you at will, that is the predicament your opponent has created by sticking. In sticking, any part of my body may be used to connect and yield to your force without disconnecting, freeing my hands to do damage. Once you touch, I just yield, and you cannot move or use force, even if you punch.

"Why not? Because human nature will always seek the tangible and substantial. Our sense of touch is reassured by the feel of solidity, and instinctively we want something solid to hold on too. That's why if I use strength or have force, you feel more comfortable; if I have no force, then you feel less comfortable. You strive to connect with

...if I use strength or have force, you feel more comfortable; if I have no force, then you feel less comfortable. You strive to connect with my solidity, and you will instinctively overextend and follow me to where you don't want go, trying to find it.

my solidity, and you will instinctively overextend and follow me to where you don't want go, trying to find it.

In sticking, move only when necessary. Don't move until pushed. Once your opponent pushes and you stick to them with your ward-off (peng), you can hit them with impunity. Because while you stick, they cannot attack, being already completely controlled; that is the true meaning of sticking."

6. Mind Games

"If you give your opponent force, he'll know you're coming. Give him no-force, and he will not know you're coming. Then you can control him with kindness. At the point of contact and the moment of touch, you confound the nervous system of your opponent by yielding, sticking, and circling the force back. Thus you achieve the ability to uproot their center and send them flying with no-force.

In confounding your opponent's nervous system...you can immediately take advantage of any strength they put out or force they use...

"In confounding the opponent's nervous system, with 99 percent of people, you can immediately take advantage of any strength they put out or force they use, whether consciously as in a push or unconsciously by leaning with the centerline. For example, if they have too much intention (strength) in their ward-off, you will know their intention and have access to their center; they're giving you a big handle to control them with.

"Above all, to do it right, you have to do it light. You have to feel your opponent's centerline, go in with delicate feeling, slipping by the obstructions, and continue all the way through it. Then, by the time they feel it, your mind is already out through their back, and they will be gone.

"You control your opponent by causing them to react—subtly varying the quality of your touch at the point of contact, either by "emptying on them" (responding with no-force) or penetrating them a little with your intention. For example, when you touch me, my force is either a little less than yours or a little more than yours, with changing pressure and intention on each point and from point to point, until you're paralyzed and uprooted.

With noodlers (a term often used to refer to folks who neutralize partially without regard to central equilibrium and with excessive movement -j.d.) , you have to realize that people become noodles and squirm only when force is used. But if awareness and no-force is used, you can go straight through them, and they will fly. If your opponent begins to noodle, your hands must stop creating force. Resist the temptation to go for it and use strength; don't let them

Fig. 12-5. Exploring the Chin Na implications of roll-back

fool you. Instead, let them build their own trap. When they move, you just lock them up; they will tense, and the noodle will become spaghetti. Once you feel that, you know they are uprooted and you put your intention through the backbone and they will fly".

7. Pattern Practice

"The purpose of any pattern practice is to have a method of practicing fundamental principles. This is true in push-hands as well as solo practice.

"First learn single-hand horizontal circle pushing. And in single push-hands, it's easier to first learn the cycle touching with the hand corresponding to the rear foot. Then learn the four variations. In right archer stance, (1) left hands touching and circling or (2) right hands touching and circling; and in left archer stance, (3) left hands touching and circling or (4) right hands touching and circling. This pattern is, above all, to train the hips to turn 45 degrees in both directions in order to physically disappear to any intended force. Be certain to turn the forearm of the ward-off into a downward push, simultaneously turning the torso 45 degrees and sinking.

I prefer Zheng Manqing's pattern to the pattern taught by Yang Shouzhong, Dong Yingjie, and many others, because it is more complete.

"For the double pattern, I use the push-hands patterns of the Zheng Manqing Yang style Taijiquan. I prefer Zheng Manqing's pattern to the pattern taught by Yang Shouzhong, Dong Yingjie, and many others, because it is more complete. The pattern of Yang Shouzhong and Dong Yingjie has ward-off, push, and rollback, but it really doesn't have a press. Therefore it's not a complete circle. Zheng Manqing's pattern is more complete, because it includes the press and requires rotational yielding to both sides.

"Zheng Manqing's traditional pushing pattern consists of two attacks and two yieldings. The first attack is the

236

Fig. 12-6. Masters Sam Tam and Fong Ha
demonstrating   the   push-hands   pattern

push, which is received by the ward-off and is deflected
45 degrees with rollback. This first yielding is countered
by the second attack of press as a continuation of the

straight force of the push. The press is countered by the second yielding, turning 45 degrees in the other direction, while covering the pressing hands of the opponent with one's own and guiding them into the void created by turning.

"In the beginning you always have to help your partner, and therefore you both profit from going very slowly and carefully, to help feeling and knowing. In the beginning practice this pattern by having your and your opponent's front feet close to each other. After a while you can align the respective front and rear feet equally. And you must learn to do all the patterns fast and slow, strong and soft, heavy and light, any way that you can imagine, thereby learning how to respond to all the different possibilities.

"So be intelligent and patient in your learning. Practice the solo version of the double pattern and be able to visualize what is happening in terms of the cycle of two attacks and two defenses.

"When you are pushed do not be concerned with having a strong protective cushion with your ward-off. It creates a tension that will be used against you; yield to their strength, stick to it, and turn it. It's all right for the elbow to collapse as needed as long as your awareness is maintained. The main thing is, when you are pushed, you must not turn too late; if you do, you will not be able to rollback, and you're gone.

"To push correctly, don't lean your centerline forward. That's using force and your opponent will know you're coming, which is no good, for they will have time

> In the beginning you always have to help your partner, and therefore you both profit from going very slowly and carefully, to help feeling and knowing.

to react and thus there will be dispute. Instead you must sink your energy straight down and straight up simultaneously with your intention moving horizontally forward through them. Then they won't feel you coming, and there will be no dispute.

"On the ward-off, when shifting back into rollback, I draw in your push on my ward-off to where the fingertips of my ward-off arm reach the elbow of my rollback arm. At that point, my body and forearm rotate to do the rollback and lead your push into emptiness. At the same time, I continue to go to the place where you don't want to go, where you will be uprooted and controlled. But I use no force. That's how you control your opponent with kindness.

"When somebody tries to push through your rollback and thereby puts force on your arm, let your body and arm yield and circle this strength back with a press.

"When you defend against the press by rotating 45 degrees to the other side, cover the opponent's pressing hands with your palm, sink, and turn your waist 45 degrees to lead their press into emptiness. At the same time, your other hand immediately slides down to control his elbow. Pay attention here that you don't grab the hand and turn too fast to respond to the press. The timing must be right: At the moment the opponent's hand presses their other one, you turn and cover it with your own. If you grab, you are using force and it tells your opponent that your hips were not turning.

The timing must be right: At the moment the opponent's hand presses their other one, you turn and cover it with your own.

"Just by straightening out the body appropriately and

turning at the right moment, the opponent is spun off with no force. That is what it means to take their energy into the backbone/spine. No matter where you push me on the outside I'm just rolling around it. On the inside I'm like a ball bearing: when you push, my body just turns. Just by my not resisting, **you** are turning **my** body, with no effort on my part.

Just by straightening out the body appropriately and turning at the right moment, the opponent is spun off with no force. That is what it means to take their energy into the backbone/spine.

"It is of great importance not to lean backward or forward while shifting back. If you lean backward, your spine and center line are broken, and you will be had. If you lean forward, it will prevent the CL from rotating 45 degrees, and you will have to use arm/hand strength to compensate; then you're gone because you're using strength, and local strength at that. If done properly, the turning is like power steering where very little strength turns a big car effortlessly. It seems so simple, but you must remember that the most profound things reside in the simplest things."

Afterword:

Martial Art as Transformative Process

The distinction between the yang and yin meanings of peng are extremely helpful in describing the developmental process of the individual martial artist. As in all athletic endeavors, personal growth in the martial arts occurs within the context of the biological aging process. When we are young, we are "full of piss and vinegar," as the old saying goes. In that prime of physical, neuro-muscular development, our strength and energies are greatest, but often our control, a function of awareness and the mind, is not. In the best possible scenario, the situation reverses as we age: though strength may wane, awareness increases.

This polarity reversal defines the three possible stages of martial and spiritual development in the martial artist. For the sake of convenience, and as a rough approximation, I will refer to these as the practitioner stage, the mastery stage and the grandmaster stage. Two profound transformations in the relationship of body and mind separate these three stages.

The practitioner stage is defined by the use of external, segmented strength derived from the momentum of movement. In the first transformation leading to the stage of mastery, this external or segmented strength is transformed into internal or integral strength, as movement is transformed into stillness.

THE TAO OF YIQUAN

In the second transformation, leading to the stage of grand-mastery, the use of force is relinquished altogether, and control over an opponent is achieved by means of awareness alone. This realm of yin-peng, as described by Grandmaster Ma, involves the complete subordination of the neuro-muscular (efferent) system to the neuro-sensory (or afferent) nervous system.

The difficulties of these transformations also account for the relative paucity of true martial arts mastery and the even rarer occurrences of true, as opposed to self-proclaimed, grand-mastery. Most practitioners are unable to sustain the disciplined practice of stillness required to transform segmented into integrated strength, and therefore remain forever stuck on the level of practitioner.

The surrender of the use of force altogether, required by the second transformation into the realm of grand-mastery, is even more difficult. Decades of emphasizing strength and force create practice habits and a corresponding mind set that are not easily discarded. As Master Tam put it:

"If you follow my methods and practice diligently, it will only take a few years to master pushing with no force. Why then do only so few martial artists, even Taiji practitioners, break through and master no-force? It is not that they don't practice enough, but that they practice too much with the wrong idea. They are too attached to lifelong habits of using strength and force to uproot and fajin their opponents; and as long as they continue to use force in their practice, they will be unable to make the breakthrough to no-force."

Afterword: Martial Art as Transformative Process

"Don't get me wrong. I know many practitioners understand the necessity for giving up force. But understanding something does not mean mastery over it. On the contrary, if you know it but you don't do it, and you keep practicing improperly, you make your wrong more wrong, and it will become even harder for you to change. Like anything else, if you don't want to give up your habits that stand in the way, it becomes more and more work to deprogram and reprogram."

Sadly, therefore, most martial art masters fail to develop beyond this level and fulfill their highest potential. But for those lucky few with egos flexible enough to surrender the old to the new, the reward is a spiritual transformation.

The acquisition of yin pengjin resolves in a profound way the spiritual and ethical paradox inherent in the acquisition of martial ability. This paradox consists of the fact that the greater the power acquired, the less it can be used. In the spiritual development of the martial artist, therefore, the knowledge of violence must beget the pledge of nonviolence. Otherwise, one is doomed to remain operating on the level of the bully. Spiritual progress in the martial artist, then, means being increasingly able to view self-defense situations as opportunities to practice compassion.

Defined by the ability to control physical conflict with minimum physical force and maximum awareness, yin pengjin produces a nonviolent, homeopathic martial art. A Master of yin pengjin dilutes all finite strengths into the greater infinity of awareness, and applies the absolute

minimum dosage of it to heal the conflict. Thus characterized by emptiness, awareness, and compassion, the supreme skill of yin pengjin represents the highest achievement in the martial arts.

Who can resist the quest?

Notes

Chapter 1

1. Tomio Nagaboshi, *The Bodhisattva Warriors* (Samuel Weiser, York Beach, ME, 1994), p.158. Much of these introductory pages are but a summary of the voluminous data presented in this seminal work.

2. Ibid., p. 161.

3. Ibid.

4. Ibid., p.162.

5. Ibid., p. 163.

6. Ibid, p. 166.

7. Ibid.

8. Ibid., p. 173.

9. Ibid., p. 188.

10. Ibid., p. 220.

11. Ibid., p. 221

12. Ibid., p. 223.

13. Ibid., p. 168.

14. Ibid.

15. Ibid., p. 173.

16. Ibid., p. 178.

17. Ibid.

18. Ibid., p. 174.

19. Ibid., pp. 216, 219.

20. Ibid., p. 179

21. Ibid., p. 223.

Chapter 2

1. Bill Porter, *The Road to Heaven: Encounters with Chinese Hermits* (San Francisco, Mercury House, 1993), pp. 88-9.

2. Ibid.

3. Arthur F. Wright, *Buddhism in Chinese History* (Stanford, CA: Stanford University Press, 1991), p. 23.

4. Ibid., p. 26.

5. Ibid.

6. Ibid., p. 27.

7. Ibid., p. 32.

8. Ibid., p. 35.

9. Ibid., p. 41.

10. Ibid., p. 42.

11. Ibid., p. 44.

12. Ibid., p. 48.

13. Ibid.

14. Ibid., p. 57.

15. Ibid., p. 67.

16. Xinru Lu, *Ancient India and Ancient China* (Oxford: Oxford University Press, 1994), p.145.

17. Tomio Nagaboshi, *The Bodhisattva Warriors* (York Beach, ME: Samuel Weiser, 1994), pp. 299, 301. See also: Yang Jwing-Ming, *Muscle/Tendon Changing and Marrow/Brain Washing Chi Kung,* (Jamaica Plains, MA: YMAA Publications Center, 1989), pp, 23-4.

18. Nagaboshi, op. cit., p. 229.

19. Ibid., 228.

20. Ibid., 231.

21. Ibid., 229.

22. Ibid., 230.

23. Ibid., 435.

24. Yang Jwing-Ming, op. cit., pp. 23-4.

25. Ibid.

26. Wright, op. cit., p. 70.

27. Nagaboshi, op. cit., p.185.

28. Ibid., p. 263.

29. Ibid., p. 225.

Notes

30. Ibid., p. 191.

31. Ibid., p. 233.

32. Ibid., pp. 209-11

33. Ibid., p. 233.

Chapter 3

1. Arthur F. Wright, *Buddhism in Chinese History* (Stanford, CA: Stanford University Press, 1991), p. 94.

2. Ibid., p. 95.

3. Liang Shou-Yu and Yang Jwing-Ming, *Hsing Yi Chuan* (Jamaica Plain, MA: YMAA Publication Center, 1990), p. 12.

4. Ibid., p. 14.

5. Ted Knecht, *Internal Arts of the Shoalin Temple*, http://home.earthlink.net/~twk/

6. Ibid.

7. Howard Reid and Michael Croucher, *The Way of the Warrior* (London: Leopard Books, 1995), p. 27.

8. Wong Kiew Kit, *Shaolin Kung Fu* (London: Paul Crompton LTD, 1996), pp. 6-7.

9. Wang Xuanjie, *Dachengquan* (Hong Kong: Hai Feng Publishing Co., Ltd.), p. 5.

10. Liang Shou-Yu and Yang Jwing-Ming, op. cit., p.14.

11. Ibid., p. 12.

12. Ibid., p. 15.

13. Tomio Nagaboshi, *The Bodhisattva Warriors* (York Beach, ME: Samuel Weiser, 1994), p. 223.

14. Sun Lu Tang, *Xing Yiquan Xue, The Study of Form-Mind Boxing* (Pacific Grove, CA: High View Publications), p. 42.

15. Nagaboshi, op.cit., p. 235.

16. E. Dale Saunders, *Mudra-- A Study of Symbolic Gestures in Japanese Buddhist Sculpture* (Princeton, NJ:

Princeton University Press, Bollingen Series LVIII, 1985),
p. 58.

17. Nagaboshi, op. cit., p.233.

18. George E. Mattson, *The Way Of Karate* (Rutland, Vt:
Charles E. Tuttle Company, 1992), p. 65.

19. Robert W. Smith, *Hsing I: Chinese Mind-Body Boxing*
(Tokyo: Kodansha International Ltd, 1974), pp. 32-3.

20. Nagaboshi, op. cit.

21. Wang Xuanjie, op. cit., p. 5.

22. Liang Shou-Yu and Yang Jwing-Ming, op. cit., p. 11.

23. Smith, op. cit., p. 10.

24. Ibid., p. 11.

25. Smith., op. cit., p.12.

26. Sun Lu Tang, op. cit., p. 14.

27. Smith., op. cit.. pp. 92-95.

Chapter 4

1. Beijing Yiquan Association , *The Record of the Life of
Wang Xiangzhai –Celebrating the 100th year of His Birth*,
1986.

2. Ibid.

3. Wang Xiangzhai, *The True Course of Yiquan*, in *Comprehensive Collection of Yi Quan Documents,* edited by
Hong Kong Yi Quan Study Society, (Hong Kong: Cosmos
Books, 1994)

4. Ibid.

5. Ibid.

6.Wang Xiangzhai, *The True Course of Yiquan*, Li Ying
Arn, ed.,(Hong Kong: Unicorn Press, 1983.

7. Ibid.

8. Beijing Yiquan Association, op. cit.

9. Ibid.

10. Arn, op. cit.

Notes

11. Beijing Yiquan Association, op. cit.

12. Ibid.

13. Ibid.

14. Arn, op. cit.

15. Ibid.

16. Beijing Yiquan Association, op. cit.

17. Ibid.

18. Ibid.

19. Ibid.

20. Ibid.

21. Wang Xuan Jie, *Dachengquan* (Hong Kong: Hai Feng Publishing Co, 1988.), p. 3.

22. Tomio Nagaboshi, *The Bodhisattva Warriors* (York Beach, ME: Samuel Weiser Publishers, 1994), p. 89.

23. Wang Xuan Jie op. cit., p. 5.

24. Kuo, Simone, *Shao-Lin Chuan –The Rhythm & Power of Tan-Tui* (Berkeley: North Atlantic Books, 1996), p. 6.

25. Arn, op. cit.

26. Ibid.

27. Personal correspondence with Ning Qiang, Ph.D., Professor of Chinese archeology, and expert on Dun Huang cave art.

28. Beijing Yiquan Association (?), op. cit.

29. Wang Hsiangzhai, op. cit.

30. Wang Xuan Jie op. cit., p. 39.

31. Ibid.

32. Sawai, Kenichi, *Taiki-Ken, the Essence of Kung-fu* (Japan Publications, Inc. 1976), p. 10.

33. Wang Xiangzhai, op. cit.

34. Ibid.

35. Beijing Yiquan Association (?), op. cit.

36. Yao Zongxun, *Seeking the Origin of Yiquan,* in *Comprehensive Collection of Yi Quan Documents,* ed-

ited by Hong Kong Yi Quan Study Society, (Hong Kong: Cosmos Books, 1994)

37. Ibid.

38. Ibid.

Chapter 6

1. Fong Ha, *Handout (Berkeley: 1997)*

2. Wang Xiangzhai, *The True Course of Yiquan*,

3. Deane Juhan, *Job's Body-A handbook for Bodywork* (New York: Station Hill Press, Inc., 1987), pp. 172,3.

4. Ibid.

5. Ibid.

Chapter 7

1. Michael Mayer, *Standing Meditation: Doing Nothing and Finding Contentment in Being Alight* (Berkeley: The Body/Mind Qigong Center, 1997), p.51.

Chapter 8

1. Wilhelm Reich, *The Function of the Orgasm* (New York: Noonday Press, 1961), pp. 263-4.

2. Wang Xuanjie, *Dacheng Kungfu* (Shanghai: China Prospect Publishing House, 1989), p.21.

Chapter 9

1. Wang Xuanjie, *Dacheng Kungfu* (Shanghai: China Prospect Publishing House, 1989), p.37.

2. Jan Diepersloot, *Warriors of Stillness, V. 1 –Qigong of the Center and the Essence of Taijiquan*, (Walnut Creek: Center For healing & The Arts, 1995)

3. Ibid., pp. 204-5.

4. Deane Juhan, *Job's Body-A handbook for Bodywork* (New York: Station Hill Press, Inc., 1987), p.116.

Notes

5. For an extended discussion of 'filling the mingmen," see Diepersloot, op. cit., pp. 13-14.

Chapter 10

1. Patrick Kelley, *Taiji Secrets* (Auckland: G&H Publications), p.138.

2. Ibid.

3. Ibid., p.139.

4. Wang Xuanjie, *Dacheng Kungfu* (Shanghai: China Prospect Publishing House, 1989), p.5.

5. Ibid.

6. Ibid.

7. Ibid., p.40.

8. Ibid.

9. Intro to Wang Xiangzhai, *The True Course of Yiquan*, Li Ying Arn, ed.,(Hong Kong: Unicorn Press, 1983.

10. Kuo Lien Ying (Guttman, transl.) *The T'ai Chi Boxing Chronicle* (Berkeley: North Atlantic Books, 1994), p.131.

11. Smith, *Chinese Boxing -Masters and Methods*, (Berkeley, CA: North Atlantic Books, 1990), p. 35.

Index

Index

Index

Index

Index

Index

O

"om" sound, 178
opening and closing polarity. *See* Closing and opening polarity
opposites and polarities, 89–90
oppositional movement of arms, 140–142
    exercises, 158–161
Ou Yang (Mme Yu Pengxi), 186(fig), 187

P

pain, 104–108
Pala dynasty (rulers of India), 9
parallel stances, 126
pattern practice, 69, 74, 236–240, 237(fig)
pelvic tilt (tucking of tailbone)
    alignment of spine, 113–114
    and breathing, 149
    in expansion from wuji center, 193–194
    and sinking of Qi, 216
    in stretching, 92
peng (frame), iii. *See also* Frame
peng (neuro-muscular realm), 197, 241. *See also* Yang-peng
peng (neuro-sensory realm), 197, 241. *See also* Yin-peng
peng polarity, 198. *See also* Yang-Yin polarity
pengjin (expanding energy), 194, 198, 243–244
perception and empty force, 203, 208
perseverance of practice, 96
perspiration test of standing meditation, 57
pile standing. *See* Zhanzhuang (pile standing)
pile (universal post) stance. *See* Universal post (pile) stance
point of contact, 229, 230, 235
polarity
    and balance of opposing forces, 183
    of centerline, 111–112
    of development of martial artist, 241
    and discharge of energy, 191–193
    in exercises, 122
    and the grammar of movement, 119–143
    of sphere, 116, 133
    as a tool of enlightenment, 89–90
    types of, 119
posture, 106–107(fig)
    attention to, 86–87
    spine alignment, 112
    in standing meditation, 104–108
    and torso, 110
    in zhuangfa, 87
power steering, strength as, 240
power training stances, 126

Index

Index

Index

Index

Data Base and Order Form

☐ Yes, enter me into your data base and keep me informed of future publications and other products

Name: _____

Address: _____

City:_____

State_____

ZIP:_____

Email: _____

☐ Also, send me ___copies of
Yiquan -The Method of Awareness in the Martial Arts
at the above address.

I enclose a check for: $_____

This was calculated as follows:

No. of books: ____x $24.95   = $_____
Shipping & handling
   ☐ U.S.: $4 for 1st book, $2 each addtional   =$_____
   ☐ Foreign: $15 for 1st book, $5 each addtional =$_____
CA residents: sales tax @ 7.25%   =$_____
Total   =$_____

Please send data/order form (and make checks payable)to:

Center For Healing & The Arts
POB 369
Walnut Creek, CA 94597

Or register or order on the Internet. Visit our webpage at www.warriorsofstillness.com